THE MELODIOUS DRUM OF DAKINI LAND

VENERABLE VAJRAYOGINI

THE MELODIOUS DRUM
OF DAKINI LAND

A Commentary to the Extensive Dedication
Prayer of Venerable Vajrayogini

Yangchen Drupai Dorje

Translated by David Gonsalez

DECHEN LING PRESS · SEATTLE · 2013

Dechen Ling Press
3633 Whitman Avenue North
Seattle WA 98103
www.dechenlingpress.org

0989223116
First Edition
Printed in the United States
ISBN-13: 978-0-9892231-1-9

Designed by Gopa & Ted2, Inc.

Contents

Special Acknowledgments

DECHEN LING PRESS would like to express our heartfelt gratitude to Lama Namdrol Tulku Rinpoche and Tekchen Choling Dharma Center in Singapore for generously funding this translation project. Their great kindness will bring immense benefit to English-speaking Vajrayana practitioners far into the future and go a long way in preserving this important lineage.

Dechen Ling Press would also like to extend our deep gratitude to all the other kind supporters of these final four publications. Together we have created something truly meaningful.

Losang Tsering (David Gonsalez)
Dechen Ling Press
Translator/Director

Translator's Introduction

THE FIRST SECTION of this book contains a commentary to the extensive dedication prayer to Vajrayogini. The commentary was composed by Yangchen Drupai Dorje (1809–1887), and the extensive dedication prayer itself, translated in the second section, was composed by the great Sakya lama Tsarchen Losal Gyatso (1502–1566). Yangchen Drupai Dorje's commentary on the dedication prayer is incredibly lucid and accessible and provides rich commentary on both the generation and completion stages. Thus it not only serves as a commentary to the dedication prayer but stands alone as a very practical commentary to the practice as a whole.

I had the great good fortune to receive the oral transmission and commentary to this text from my guru Gen Lobsang Choephel (b. 1928), who himself has dedicated his entire life to the practice of Vajrayogini. He entered Ganden Kachoe Monastery in the Laylung district of Tibet at the age of five and within a decade had received the empowerment and commentary of Vajrayogini. While at Ganden Kachoe, he accomplished numerous retreats of varying lengths until he was exiled from Tibet at approximately thirty-five years of age. He then spent nineteen years in solitary retreat and subsequently became the textual scribe for, and close disciple of, Kyabje Trijang Rinpoche (1901–1981). During his six years at the private residence of Trijang Rinpoche, he received the empowerment and commentary of Vajrayogini numerous times, both privately and publicly, and accomplished the retreat once again under Trijang Rinpoche's guidance. Thus he is a treasure of scripture and realization.

It is my hope that this book will go a long way in helping to spread the practice of Vajrayogini to English-speaking initiates and that they will thereby all come under the loving care of Guru-Vajrayogini and swiftly attain outer and inner Dakini Land.

Acknowledgments

FIRST AND FOREMOST I would like to express my deep gratitude to Gen Lobsang Choephel, who kindly gave me all the empowerments, transmissions, and commentaries to this amazing practice. I would also like to extend my deepest gratitude to Lama Zopa Rinpoche, Kyabje Ribur Rinpoche, Geshe Khenrab Gajam and all of my other gurus that have guided me along my spiritual path. I would like to thank Susan and David Heckerman, whose continued support allows me the opportunity to spend all of my time dedicated to practice, study, translation, and teaching. I am also grateful to the members of Dechen Ling Buddhist Center who assist me in accomplishing my various activities, especially Karolyn McKinley, Kirk Wilson, Guru Dorje, and others. I would like to extend my belated thanks to Thubten Jinpa, Glenn Mullin, and Gelek Rinpoche for their very generous and glowing endorsements of my earlier, related translation of Pabongkha Dechen Nyingpo's *Extremely Secret Dakini of Naropa: Vajrayogini Practice and Commentary* (Snow Lion, 2011), which unfortunately did not appear on the dust jacket. I would like to extend my gratitude to Sharpa Tulku for his continued support and friendship and for going over a few of the difficult passages of the present work with me, which was very helpful. Special thanks to Andy Weber for the line drawings in the text, including the frontispiece. I would also like to thank my dear friend the late Wolfgang Saumweber and his wife Linda for the following graphics: placement of body-mandala deities *within* the central channel, the syllable BAM's stages of dissolution, the armor mantra placement, and the armor mantra-syllables with explanations. I would like to thank the staff at the Tibetan Buddhist Research Center (TBRC) as well as its founder, the late and great Gene Smith, for their constant support in providing me with texts needed for my various projects and for the invaluable service that they provide. I would also like to extend my gratitude to Sidney Piburn, one of the cofounders of Snow Lion Publications, who has been an invaluable ally in bringing this and other books to fruition while constantly providing his unwavering support. In addition, I thank Chris Banigan for his cover design and my editor, Victoria R. M. Scott, for her dedication and expertise.

All the royalties from this and all other translation projects are donated to Ganden Kachoe Monastery, Gen Lobsang Choephel's monastery in Southern India.

Losang Tsering (David Gonsalez)
Seattle, December 2013

Technical Note

THERE IS A growing and legitimate movement among Tibetan translators to present the Sanskrit in mantras in a way that transliterates the original Sanskrit characters into English characters. A transliteration converts a word written in the alphabet of one writing system into that of another; for example, it converts a word written in Devanagari script into one using the Roman alphabet. In the case of Sanskrit transliteration, this requires adding diacritical marks to some of the characters in the Roman alphabet so as to be able to distinguish all the vowels and consonants of Sanskrit. Thus, from the transliteration into English of a Sanskrit word, someone familiar with Devanagari should be able to reconstruct the spelling of the Sanskrit word in Devanagari.

The goal of transliteration per se is to translate the written alphabetic characters of one language into those of another, not to render the *sounds* of the language. Sometimes a transliteration system also aims to achieve a partial phonetic rendering of the words. By selecting characters whose pronunciations in the target language are similar to those of the characters in the source language, one can get transliterations that also approximate the way the word should be pronounced, as, for example, in the transliteration of Russian Cyrillic script into Roman letters. In the case of Sanskrit transliterations using diacritics, the transliterations guide correct pronunciation only if one knows how the various vowels and consonants in the transliteration should be pronounced. For example, one needs to know that in Sanskrit the "c" in "bodhicitta" is pronounced "ch." Thus a more phonetic transliteration would be "bodhichitta." Not all transliterations have phonetic rendering as a goal. The Wylie system of transliterating Tibetan into English does not, which is why Tibetan transliterations using Wylie look so bizarre and unpronounceable to readers unfamiliar with it; for example, 'jig rten grags pa is pronounced "Jigten Dragpa."

The situation gets quite complicated with the Sanskrit mantras found in Tibetan Buddhist sadhanas. The Tibetan masters who received tantras from India recognized that there was power in the Sanskrit phonemes of the mantras, and thus tried to achieve a transliteration that gave some guidance as to how the Sanskrit should be pronounced. But they also tried to transliterate the Sanskrit characters into Tibetan script with the goal of strict transliteration in mind, that is, translating Sanskrit written characters into Tibetan written characters. At the same time, there developed an oral tradition, transmitted from master to student, of how these Sanskrit mantras, now transliterated into Tibetan script, should be pronounced. In some cases, the Tibetan pronunciation differed from the Indian pronunciation. For example, the word transliterated into English as "Vajrasattva" was transliterated into Tibetan correctly but was sometimes pronounced "Benzra satto." This was partly due to the fact that Tibetan doesn't have the phoneme /v/.

Translators of Tibetan Buddhist sadhanas and commentaries are thus faced with a daunting task. The mantras in the written text are Tibetan transliterations of Sanskrit mantras, which partially transliterate the written Sanskrit of the original mantras into Tibetan script. These need to be rendered in English. But translators must also take into account the Tibetan oral tradition, in which the way to recite these mantras has been transmitted unbrokenly from masters to disciples for hundreds of years. Translators must thus try to balance the need to render the Sanskrit in these sadhanas in such a way that (a) the Sanskrit words are recognizable (this aids in translating the meaning of the mantras into English), (b) English readers without knowledge of scholarly Sanskrit transliteration that uses diacritics will have a good chance of pronouncing the Sanskrit as it would have been pronounced by an ancient Indian Buddhist, and (c) English readers without knowledge of the oral Tibetan tradition will have a good chance of pronouncing the mantras as they have been transmitted orally by their Tibetan teachers. The latter task is made even more difficult by the fact that there are differences in the way Tibetans pronounce the mantras, differences due to (a) regional differences in Tibetan dialects, (b) differences between practice traditions associated with different monasteries (for example, there are differences between the way the monks of Gyuto and Gyume monasteries recite the same mantras even though these monasteries are both Gelug), and (c) differing degrees to which these Tibetan masters are trying to pronounce the Sanskrit as modern-day Sanskrit scholars would pronounce them.

One other factor that translators must take into account is that, in the last thirty years, certain conventions in rendering these Sanskrit mantras into English have become more entrenched. For example, in the mantra DZA HUM BAM HO, a more correct transliteration would be DZA HUM VAM HO. That is, in the case of the third word of the mantra, V is a better rendering of the Sanskrit written character than is B, so VAM would be a more accurate transliteration. But if BAM is closer to the way Tibetan masters pronounce it, and for the last thirty years all the sadhanas use BAM, should it now be changed to VAM just because this is a better transliteration of the Sanskrit?

Translators have not generally opted for a purely phonetic rendering of the Sanskrit mantras. There is still some need to indicate what the written Sanskrit characters would be. For example, the Sanskrit term PHAT is regularly used. If the term were to be rendered completely phonetically (as pronounced by Tibetans), it would be spelled PAY. But hardly any translators use PAY because they don't want to lose sight of the transliteration goal. It is rendered as PHAT because the H is supposed to indicate that the P is pronounced with a strong aspiration, and because there is a Sanskrit character at the end of the word that is transliterated as T. So PHAT is partially a transliteration and partially a phonetic rendering. PHAT is not a wholly phonetic rendering; it can easily lead to a mispronunciation as FAT since the PH in English is sounded as F. One must know the conventions governing the pronunciation of these hybrid spellings in order to pronounce them as intended.

In sum, an accurate transliteration of the mantras requires using diacritics but offers no guidance in itself as to how the mantras *sound*, yet there are no transliterations that are wholly or partially phonetic renderings that will satisfy everyone either, since there are so many different pronunciations even by those within established practice traditions. Since this volume is designed to be useful to practitioners, I have spelled the mantras phonetically in the commentary in such a way that they accord with the way my lama pronounces them, even though this might be considered inaccurate by a Sanskrit scholar. I have also relied on some of the spelling conventions that have been used by other translators of Tibetan Buddhist sadhanas and associated texts. Thus many consonants are followed by an H to indicate a more breathy sound, as in PHAT, DHUPE, and BHAGAVAN, although SH is pronounced as it is in the English word "ship"! An E, especially when it is the final letter of a word, is pronounced more like AY, so DHUPE is pronounced "DHUPAY," ME is pronounced "MAY," and so forth. Sometimes there are striking differences between the way a mantra is pronounced by Tibetans and the way the Sanskrit would be pronounced by a Sanskrit scholar. For example, in the Vajrasattva mantra, the more accurate transliteration of two of the phrases would be SUTOSHYO ME BHAVA, SUPOSHYO ME BHAVA, yet many Tibetans pronounce this SUTO KAYO ME BHAWA, SUPO KAYO ME BHAWA. Since there are so many factors that affect the way these mantras are recited by Tibetan teachers (lineage traditions, regional dialects, and so forth), it is important for practitioners to learn to pronounce them in accordance with the wishes of their lama or a qualified teacher in the tradition.

With respect to the Tibetan terms, I have used phonetic renderings, with the transliteration of important terms, titles, and persons presented in footnotes using the Wylie system. I have also kept the footnotes at an absolute minimum, using them only when I felt the text would be difficult to understand without them. Since this text is a commentary intended for practitioners, it is not academic in style and does not rely heavily upon citing quotations and so forth; therefore, the minimalist approach to the footnotes is in keeping with the style of the commentary itself.

With respect to the outline of the text, although it will not meet the standards of Western academia, I have retained the format of the original Tibetan. Although some might consider the Tibetan style of outlining a text rather primitive and oversimplistic, the structure is designed to allow for ease in memorization and recitation. Once memorized, it provides immediate access to the overall structure of the commentary as well as its subheadings without the need to resort to a printed text, which can be highly beneficial both in meditation and as a teaching aid.

A Brief Biography of
Yangchen Drupai Dorje (1809–1887)

As for Yangchen Drupai Dorje Losang Chöphel's place of birth, from among the three—Ü, Tsang, and Kham[1]—he was born in Tsang, near Tashi Gemphel Ling. In earlier times, this place was called Je, but later, since Padmasambhava had smiled three times when he visited it, the name of the place was changed to Shay (meaning "smile") as a good omen. Yangchen Drupai Dorje was born to Ngulchu Dharmabhadra's [1772–1851] younger brother Tashi and his wife Tsering Sichö, during the fourteenth rabjung[2] in the Earth Snake year of 1809, on the evening of the fifth day of the tenth month, among numerous wondrous signs.

In 1813, at the age of five, he received the commentary on grammar and the oral transmission of the Situ text from his uncle, the all-knowing [Ngulchu] Dharmabhadra, and he began learning the alphabet. At that time his name was Jamyang Dorje, and at only six years of age, he had engaged in extensive studies with various lamas and excelled in learning and memorization, completing everything without obstruction.

In 1818, in his tenth year, near the cave of Lama Losang, in another cave, called Gyamo Trapuk, there was a lama named Tobgyel Lama Ngawang Nyendrak, from whom Yangchen Drupai Dorje received many teachings. All the favorable conditions for living were given to him by Kuwo Chösang. There he studied astrology and charts, thus memorizing all the descriptions of everything [necessary for astrology]. At that time

1. Ü is in Central Tibet, Kham is in Eastern Tibet, and Tsang is in Western Tibet.
2. A rabjung is a sixty-year cycle. Thus the fourteenth rabjung is 840 years since the establishment of the current system of the Tibetan calendar. Thanks to Glenn Mullin for this information.

his maternal grandmother, who had a great deal of affection for him, passed away. Therefore, when his grandmother passed away, he went home for a short while.

When he returned again, he began listening and contemplating with great enthusiasm. In 1819, at the age of eleven, when all the monks related to Tashi Gephel Monastery had assembled, he was accepted into the monastery. Gachen Könchok Chöphel performed the hair-cutting ceremony, and he received the name Losang Chöphel.

In 1820, at the age of twelve, in the Iron Dragon year, he received the layperson's vows and the novice monk's vows from Gachen Kön-chok Chöphel. At that point he began reading Milarepa's biography, his spiritual songs, and so forth. In this way he studied many texts. When he read the *Hundred Thousand Songs of Milarepa*, his faith and pure view were greatly increased.

In 1827, at the age of nineteen, Lama Chösang accepted him as his disciple. Beginning with language, astrology, poetry, grammar, and so forth, he then began listening, contemplating, and meditating on the great texts of sutra and tantra. He also trained in measurements of sand and three-dimensional mandalas and so forth, studying them extensively.

In 1842, at the age of thirty-four, in the Water Tiger year, he studied poems and Sanskrit with his lama and passed the exams perfectly, thus pleasing his lama, who said to him, "You did excellently." He presented him with a long khata and then gave him the name Yangchen Drupai Dorje.[3] From that point on, his name gained great renown and his fame spread.

At the age of thirty-four, on the fifteenth day of the fourth month, he received the vows of a fully ordained monk (bhikshu). He received the commentary on the bhikshu vows and the cycle of profound teach-ings on the Vinaya and, like a vast ocean, he trained purely in the moral discipline. Next, he gradually received all the profound teachings from his lama, like one vase filling another, and eventually he received them all. He then compiled all the teachings of his lama [Ngulchu Dharma-bhadra] and composed works on some of them. In between he did the

---

3. The Tibetan word "Yangchen" is a translation of "Sarasvati," the name of the goddess of poetry and language. Thus his guru named him "Accomplished One—Sarasvati Vajra," an extremely flattering way of expressing his accomplishment in language and poetry.

retreat of the supreme deity and fulfilled the needs of many people by giving empowerments and commentaries.

In 1851, at the age of forty-three, during the fourteenth rabjung in the Iron Pig year, on the eighth day of the fourth month, his kind lama [Ngulchu Dharmabhadra] dissolved his appearance back into the dharmakaya [or truth body]. Up to this point he had lived with his lama for twenty-four years without being separated from him, and thus he was quite upset at the loss of his lama. Therefore, he built a reliquary for his lama's remains and built a silver stupa, and thus perfectly completed his [lama's] wishes.

From this point on, he upheld the responsibility of being a lama throughout the monastery, building new statues as well as giving extensive teachings. Not only that, but he also published his lama's complete teachings and made corrections to them.

In 1869, at the age of sixty-one, in the fifteenth rabjung of the Earth Dragon year, he traveled to Sakya, Tashi Lhunpo, and Lhasa. In central Tibet he made prostrations and offerings to all the sacred objects. He gave advice to all the great lamas of the three monasteries as well as one of the cabinet members. Again and again he gave the nectar of the Dharma to them all.

After more than one year in central Tibet, in 1870, in the Earth Horse year, in his sixty-second year, he returned to the great monasteries and once again gave teachings. He raised high the victory banner of the Gelug lineage of teaching and practice. All the great scholars of the Land of Snow held him as their crown ornament.

In 1887, at the age of seventy-six, in the fifteenth rabjung of the Fire Pig year, on the sixteenth day of the tenth month, as he passed away, he showed the complete aspect of being a holy being. Spending his entire life working for the Dharma, his life is without comparison.

He had many disciples, including Drakchen Ngawang Tsultrim, Gongma Lharampa Gendun Gyatso, Lama Yeshe Chöphel, Mindröl Nominhen, Chabdo Phakpa Lha, Chusang Hutoktu, Laylungma Lama Tsultrim Gyaltsen,[4] Losang Jigmé, and so forth.

---

4. Lama Tsultrim Gyaltsen was the founder of Gen Lobsang Choephel's monastery Zephuk Ganden Kahoe in Tibet in 1873; Dechen Ling Center (www.dechenling.org) raised the funds for its reconstruction. It is currently located in Southern India on the Kollegal Tibetan settlement.

The compilation of his collected works contains seventy-seven texts and constitutes three volumes. As written in the request to the maha-mudra lineage lamas of the Ganden Oral Lineage:

> Your great eyes of unobservable compassion never close.
> Your vast and profound wisdom is like that of Manjushri.
> To Yangchen Drupai Dorje I make request.

COLOPHON

Composed by Zephuk Gelong Lobsang Choephel.

PART 1:

The Commentary

An Abundant Explanation of the Words and Meaning
of the Entire [Dedication] Prayer for the Path
of Naropa's Powerful Goddess of Dakini Land,
Venerable Vajrayogini, Entitled *The Deity's Melodious*
Drum Summoning One to Dakini Land

(rJe btsun rdo rje rnal 'byor ma Naro mkha' spyod dbang mo'i
lam gyi smon lam cha tshang ba'i tshig don lgug par bshad pa mkha'
sbyod zhing du 'bod pa'i lha'i rda dbyang)

Introductory Verses

The supreme deity binding all wheels that are objects of knowledge,
Inseparable from my kind guru appearing as the
All-pervasive sphere of reality of the pure mandala,
With a liberating net of a hundred light rays of great bliss,
I request you to bestow virtue and excellence.

From the devotional deeds of the fortunate,
The amazing formation of simultaneously born bliss and emptiness
Appears as the Joyous Goddess of Dakini Land in the attractive
    form of the goddess,
Dispelling their longing while caring for them until enlightenment.

I respectfully prostrate to the Panchen Naropa,
The powerful siddha who clarified the quick path like no one
    before him;
Amidst an infallible rosary of scholars and siddhas of India,
The lofty brilliance of your scripture and realization outshines
    them all.

I prostrate with my head to the feet of Je [Tsarchen] Losal Gyatso,
Who completely dispels the suffering of his fortunate disciples,
The jewel ornament that is the essence of the ocean of instructions
Of the Vajra Queen as the heart-essence of the Powerful Siddha
    [Naropa].

I shall explain the meaning and words of the prayers of
    accomplishment
That are like a tree whose branches are weighed down by the leaves
    and fruits of the complete path,

As a blossoming lotus of supplication that is
[Swarmed] by a festival of excellent bees.

FURTHERMORE, the Supreme Conqueror the Great Fifth [Dalai Lama]
stated:

> Ah Ho! No other scholars and siddhas from other lineages
> Are capable of grasping this sweet scent of
> The complete Hearing Lineage with four qualifications taught
>   by Naropa
> That arose from the mouth of the goddess and Dakini.

Among all the pandits and siddhas of the Land of Aryas, the one with
the good qualities of scholarship and attainment who is like a precious
jewel on the peak of a victory banner was the Great Lord Naropa, who
received these oral instructions directly from the Venerable Mother her-
self. The stages of the path of the Venerable Mother were extracted from
a portion of the extremely profound teachings that were hidden in the
root and explanatory tantras of Glorious Chakrasamvara. The teachings
were then transmitted to the Nepalese Pamtingpa brothers, who in turn
transmitted them in succession to their Indian and Tibetan disciples until
they reached the Venerable Sakyapa [Sachen] Kunga Nyingpo the Great
[1092–1158]. This foremost being himself was the very best of those who
attained complete mastery in these ocean-like oral instructions, which
are classified as one of the well-known "Thirteen Golden Dharmas of
the Sakyapas" or "Fourteen Golden Dharmas of Lupa,"[5] which cannot
pass beyond the iron wall of the Sakya, of which the cycle of the three
red goddesses is like the principal [deity].[6] These [instructions] accomplish the supreme attainments by which the common [ones] are [also]
accomplished. Through the accomplishment of the supreme principal,

5. Alex Berzin surmised that this is a lineage stemming from the abbots of the Ngor Monastery
subsect of the Sakya tradition, who hold the title Luding Khen Rinpoche. His theory was later
confirmed by Lama Kunga Thartse Rinpoche (b. 1935), a Sakya lama whose center, Ewam
Choden, is in Kensington, California.
6. The three principal red goddesses of the Thirteen Golden Dharmas are Indra Kachö, Maitri
Kachö, and Naro Kachö.

one attains the secondary common attainments, for which there is an inner classification that is renowned as the "Cycle of the Three Red Goddesses" or "Cycle of the Three Dakinis."

The Great Fifth [Dalai Lama] stated:

> Those with the best and intermediate faculties travel to the
>   Dakini Land with this body.
> Those with the least [fortune] will go to Dakini Land in the
>   intermediate state
> And will be transferred there with great speed in the very
>   moment of their death.
> At the very least they will discover attainments through a series
>   of rebirths.

These profound instructions are much more profound than even the profound. In the definitive sense, [Vajrayogini] is inseparable from Glorious Heruka, and in the interpretive sense, for the appearance factor, she appears as an ordinary being endowed with the two qualities of scholarship and attainment for disciples.[7] Venerable Father and Mother care for [these disciples,] and they are led to the higher states of attainment, which are transmitted by none other than the holy guru.

Here I shall present a concise explanation supplementing the literal meaning of the teachings of Tsarchen Dorje Chang the Great, entitled *A Staircase for the Fortunate Ascending to Dakini Land*.

For this, there are two sections:

1) IDENTIFYING THE VIRTUE TO BE DEDICATED
2) THE ACTUAL WAY TO DEDICATE THE VIRTUE THAT HAS
    BEEN IDENTIFIED

---

7. This is in reference to Vajrayogini appearing as a qualified guru.

Identifying the Virtue to Be Dedicated

This is revealed [in the first two lines of the dedication prayer,] which state:

> Thus, through the power of meditating properly on the perfect liberating path
> Of the Powerful Goddess of Dakini Land, the Mother of the Conquerors...

Furthermore, your main focus is any appropriate virtue that you have created as the object of dedication, for which you should think, "May this become the cause of that [which is expressed in the verse above]." Regarding the prayer, it serves as both a dedication and a prayer. Until you accomplish the goal for which you are dedicating your virtue, thinking "May this function to accomplish this [goal]" is said to be a prayer and not a dedication. Next, there is both a dedication and a prayer and that which is not a prayer and not a dedication. From among these two, this [prayer] is the former.

Furthermore, the term "Thus" means that the object immediately transcends the conventional[8] and the act of immediately dedicating the virtue from the previous practice. Because her appearance is the very embodiment of the exalted wisdom of the nondual bliss and emptiness of all the buddhas, she is the "Mother of the Conquerors," and because she externally assumes the behavior of Queen of Pure Dakini Land, she is the "Powerful Goddess." In this way, this special personal deity functions to ripen your mental continuum through the eleven yogas of the generation stage. And once it [i.e., your mental continuum] is ripened, it functions to liberate you through the instructions on the completion stage of the central channel.

The four characteristics of the Hearing Lineage are: 1) the stream of empowerment has not declined, 2) the lineage of blessing has not deteriorated, 3) the teachings are not disorderly, and 4) you are satiated by faith and respect. These also possess the four factors of validity:

---

8. The word "Thus" refers to the first word in the dedication prayer.

1) valid guru, 2) valid oral transmission, 3) valid commentary, and 4) valid experience. Thus you are identifying the virtue that is the object of dedication by saying, "In dependence upon the force of dedicating the roots of virtue that stem from practicing such oral instructions coming from a holy guru possessing an unmistaken lineage, ..."

The Actual Way to Dedicate the Virtue That Has Been Identified has four sections:

1) PRAYING TO BE CARED FOR BY A HOLY VIRTUOUS FRIEND
   WHO IS THE ROOT OF THE PATH
2) PRAYING TO GENERATE REALIZATIONS OF THE ACTUAL
   PATH IN YOUR MENTAL CONTINUUM
3) THE CONCISE MEANING OF THE COMPLETE PATH
4) PROCLAIMING WORDS OF TRUTH FOR THE SAKE OF ACCOM-
   PLISHING THE PRAYER

Praying to Be Cared for by a Holy Virtuous Friend Who Is the Root of the Path

The [last two lines of the first verse in the] dedication prayer state:

> May I properly please the qualified guru—the source of
> attainments—
> And come under his [or her] care without ever being apart.

All the sutras and tantras as well as their commentaries state that the guru is the root and source of all attainments, such as the state of a buddha as the supreme attainment, and of the common attainments, such as the eight great attainments, the four actions, and so forth. Regarding this point, from the sutra perspective, there are ten qualities, such as "pacified," "subdued," and so forth,⁹ and from the Mantra perspective

9. Regarding the ten qualities of a Mahayana guru, Kanchen Yeshe Gyaltsen's Lama Chopa commentary states: "Thus, your spiritual master should have the following ten qualities: 1) 'Subdued' through his training in moral discipline. 2) 'Pacified' through his training in concentration. 3) 'Thoroughly pacified' through his training in wisdom. 4) Possesses good qualities of

there are the twenty qualities, such as the outer and inner.[10] Once you induce certainty in these teachings, which state that you should only rely properly in thought and deed upon a holy guru who is endowed with all of these aforementioned qualifications, you are praying, "May I please my guru with my faith and devotion, and in particular practice in accordance with his [or her] teachings without ever displeasing his [or her] mind, and may I never displease him [or her] for even an instant and instead delight him [or her] until I attain enlightenment."

Praying to Generate Realizations of the Actual Path in Your Mental Continuum has two sections:

> 1) PRAYING FOR A FULLY QUALIFIED PHYSICAL BASIS AS THE PRACTITIONER
> 2) PRAYING TO RIPEN THE MENTAL CONTINUUM OF THOSE PRACTITIONERS FOR REALIZATIONS OF THE PATH

---

scripture and realization superior to your own. 5) Have great diligence in accomplishing the two aims. 6) Have a wealth of scripture through listening to numerous teachings on the three baskets. 7) Have a realization of suchness concerning the mode of existence of phenomena. 8) Be skilled in explaining instructions to his disciples. 9) Have great compassion for living beings in general and disciples in particular. 10) Does not grow weary of working for the welfare of his disciples." See Kanchen Yeshe Gyaltsen, *Manjushri's Innermost Secret: A Profound Commentary to the Practice of Lama Chopa*, forthcoming from Dechen Ling Press.

10. Regarding the twenty qualities of a tantric guru, pp. 239–41 of the Tibetan text of Kanchen Yeshe Gyaltsen's Lama Chopa commentary state: "Regarding the ten inner qualities, they are: 1) Skill in expelling through meditating on the protection circle. 2) Skill in expelling through drawing mandalas and binding them to the body and so forth. 3) Skill in bestowing the vase empowerment and the secret empowerment. 4) Skill in bestowing the wisdom–exalted-wisdom empowerment and the fourth empowerment. 5) Skill in separating enemies from their protectors and separating the conjoined. 6) Skill in torma rituals. 7) Skill in the various types of recitation such as mental recitation, vajra recitation and commitment recitation, palanquin recitation, fierce recitation, wrathful recitation, heap recitation, and so forth. 8) Skill in the means of performing wrathful actions of dispersal when they cannot be accomplished properly. 9) Skill in the ritual of consecration. 10) Skill in making ritual offerings to the mandala. The ten outer qualities are: 1) Skill in how to draw the outer mandalas and how to meditate on the inner mandalas. 2) Skill in the concentrations such as the initial preparation and so forth. 3) Skill in the hand mudras. 4) Skill in the ritual dances such as with his right leg outstretched, left leg outstretched, circular, equal posture and so forth. 5) Skill in sitting in the vajra posture, the posture of Vajrasattva, and so forth. 6) Skill in proclaiming mantras. 7) Skill in burnt offerings. 8) Skill in the offering rituals. 9) Skill in ritual actions. 10) Skill in requesting [the buddhas] to depart and summoning them back."

Praying for a Fully Qualified Physical Basis as the Practitioner has two sections:

1) PRAYING TO BECOME FULLY QUALIFIED TO BE SUITABLE TO ENTER THE RIPENING PATH
2) PRAYING TO BECOME FULLY QUALIFIED TO BE SUITABLE TO ENTER THE LIBERATING PATH

Praying to Become Fully Qualified to Be Suitable to Enter the Ripening Path has two sections:

1) PRAYING TO GENERATE THE PATHS OF THE SMALL AND MIDDLING BEINGS IN YOUR MENTAL CONTINUUM
2) PRAYING TO GENERATE THE PATH OF A GREAT BEING IN YOUR MENTAL CONTINUUM

Praying to Generate the Paths of the Small and Middling Beings in Your Mental Continuum

This is expressed in the dedication prayer, which states:

> May I be liberated from this terrifying ocean of samsara
> In the great ship of freedoms and endowments,
> Flying the white sail of being mindful of impermanence and
> Blown by the favorable winds of adopting and forsaking cause
> and effect.

We have obtained a human life of leisure and endowment and are free from the eight states of nonleisure that don't provide any opportunity to practice Dharma, such as the adverse conditions associated with the hell realms and so forth, and we have the actual favorable conditions—or something very similar to them—such as the five personal endowments and the five endowments related to others.[11] This [human body of leisure

11. The eight freedoms are freedom from being born as 1) a hell being, 2) a hungry ghost, 3) an animal, 4) an ordinary god, 5) in a country without Dharma, and 6) freedom from remaining in a country without Dharma, 7) freedom from having mental and physical impediments, and 8) freedom from holding wrong views. The five personal endowments are: 1) being born a

and endowment] is difficult to find, and having found it, you can accomplish all your temporary and ultimate needs and wishes, making it similar
to a great ship that can enter the ocean, by means of contemplating the
nine reasons associated with death, which are divided into three sets of
three. There are three roots: 1) death is certain, 2) the time of death is
uncertain, and 3) at the time of death, nothing but the Dharma will be
of any benefit. These induce the certainty: 1) to practice Dharma, 2) that
you must also practice Dharma in this very moment, and 3) that you
make the determination to only practice the Dharma [and each of these
three has three contemplations, for a total of nine]. Being mindful of
death and impermanence through these nine rounds of impermanence
is a "white sail" and is a powerful incentive to extract the essence of this
life. Only happiness will come as a result of your reliance upon engaging in virtuous actions, and only suffering will come as a result of your
performance of nonvirtue. Once you induce certainty with respect to
these and other points [concerning actions and their effects] through
numerous avenues, you will abandon the most subtle negative actions [or
misdeeds] and will adopt the practice of the most subtle virtue. Thus you
are praying, "In dependence upon being blown by this 'favorable wind,'
may I be able to liberate all beings—both myself and others—from the
terrifying, unceasing torments of the three sufferings and from this
deep and boundless great ocean of samsara." These are called "the four
common preliminaries of the path."[12]

Praying to Generate the Path of a Great Being in Your Mental Continuum

This is expressed in the dedication prayer, which states:

---

human, 2) being born in a country with Dharma, 3) being born in a country where the Dharma
is flourishing, 4) not having committed any of the five actions that prompt immediate retribu-
tion, and 5) having faith in the Buddha's teachings. The five environmental endowments are:
6) taking birth in a world where the Buddha has appeared, 7) taking birth in a world where the
Buddha taught, 8) taking birth in a world where pure Dharma is still being taught, 9) taking
birth in a world where there are people practicing Dharma, and 10) taking birth in a world
where there are benefactors for Dharma practitioners.

12. The four common preliminaries are: 1) a human life of leisure and endowment, 2) death
and impermanence, 3) the suffering of samsara, and 4) the wish for liberation.

Through the influential force of compassion for mother sentient
    beings,
May I don the armor of the magnificent bodhichitta,
Enter the deep ocean of the bodhisattva's deeds,
And become a suitable vessel for the ripening empowerment.

Just as you experience the unceasing suffering of being buffeted about
due to having fallen into the great ocean of samsara, so you come to see
that mother living beings who have cared for you with kindness since
beginningless time are also experiencing the same [suffering], due to
which you become overwhelmed with love and great compassion for
others that thinks, "How wonderful it would be if they were liberated
from their suffering." You are contemplating, "I shall attain the state of
enlightenment so that I may dispel the suffering and accomplish the happiness of living beings," which is donning the powerful armor of aspiring and engaging bodhichitta. You ripen your own mental continuum
through the six transcendent perfections and ripen the mental continuum
of others through the four ways of gathering [disciples]. Thus you are
praying, "Through entering the depths of the extremely vast, ocean-like
activities of a bodhisattva, may I become a suitable vessel for receiving
the four ripening empowerments that are the gateway of the Vajrayana."

Praying to Become Fully Qualified to Be Suitable to Enter the Liberating Path

This is expressed in the dedication prayer, which states:

Through the kindness of the qualified vajra-holder,
May I become a suitable vessel for meditating on the liberating
    path
Through enjoying the glorious nectar-blessings of
The highest yoga tantra empowerments of the Venerable Mother.

Thus, through engaging in the preliminary of purifying your mental
continuum through the common path, you should definitely enter the
path of highest yoga tantra. You cannot attain enlightenment through

the path of the Perfection Vehicle and the three lower classes of tantra alone, but eventually everyone must rely upon highest yoga tantra alone to attain enlightenment. Such a vajra-holder holds in his [or her] hands a vajra, as the sign of the interpretive meaning that symbolizes the definitive meaning of "vajra," which is that his [or her] mental continuum has completely mastered the exalted wisdom of inseparable bliss and emptiness. Therefore, the best situation would be to receive any of the Father Teachings of Heruka in the lineages of Luipa, Nagpopa, or Ghantapa, and the Mother Teachings of the thirty-seven or thirteen Varahis from a kind vajra-master who is inseparable from Vajradhara. The middling situation would be the four transmissions of Hevajra. The least would be to receive the fully qualified four empowerments in the mandala of any highest yoga tantra practice. Thus you are praying, "May I become a suitable vessel for meditation on the path as the liberating path of the generation and completion stages, through enjoying the glorious nectar of perfectly obtaining the blessing of the four empowerments in the sindhura mandala of this tradition, by utilizing the system of identifying my body, speech, and mind; the body, speech, and mind of the Venerable Mother; and the three secrets of the Yogini with the wish to continuously practice."

Furthermore, the previous beings [i.e., gurus from the past] have said that to make you suitable to partake in the blessing [empowerment] of the Venerable Mother, you should have received any of the empowerments of Mother Tantra, and to be suitable to meditate on the liberating path of the generation and completion stages, you should have received the blessing [of Vajrayogini]. Also, Je Takphu [Garwang Chökyi Wangchug, also known as Pemavajra (1876–1935)] states, "Following the teachings that accord with this explanation, it is illogical that a person must obtain the complete empowerment to be suitable to enter the ripening path. This is because the sindhura blessing does not perform the function of making you suitable to initially enter the door of highest yoga tantra. It is also my own position that you should rely upon the Solitary Father [Heruka] and so forth as the ripening agent." This states that you should obtain any appropriate empowerment[13] of Mother Tantra. Changkya [Rolpai

13. The phrase "and so forth" indicates other great empowerments of Mother Tantra.

Dorje] Rinpoche [1717–1786] states that, at a minimum, it is suitable to obtain any highest yoga tantra empowerment.

Praying to Ripen the Mental Continuum of Those Practitioners for Realizations of the Path has two sections:

1) PRAYING TO DEVELOP REALIZATIONS OF THE GENERATION STAGE IN YOUR MENTAL CONTINUUM
2) PRAYING TO DEVELOP REALIZATIONS OF THE COMPLETION STAGE IN YOUR MENTAL CONTINUUM

Praying to Develop Realizations of the Generation Stage in Your Mental Continuum has two sections:

1) PRAYING TO DEVELOP THE PATH OF THE GENERATION STAGE IN YOUR MENTAL CONTINUUM
2) PRAYING TO ACCOMPLISH THE RESULTS OF THE GENERATION STAGE

Praying to Develop the Path of the Generation Stage in your Mental Continuum has eight sections:

1) PRAYING FOR THE THREE YOGAS OF SLEEPING, RISING, AND EXPERIENCING NECTAR
2) PRAYING FOR THE TWO YOGAS OF THE IMMEASURABLES AND THE GURU
3) PRAYING FOR THE YOGA OF GENERATING ONESELF AS THE DEITY
4) PRAYING FOR THE YOGA OF PURIFYING MIGRATING BEINGS
5) PRAYING FOR THE YOGA OF BEING BLESSED BY THE HEROES AND HEROINES
6) PRAYING FOR THE YOGA OF VERBAL RECITATION AND MENTAL RECITATION
7) PRAYING FOR THE YOGA OF INCONCEIVABILITY
8) PRAYING FOR THE YOGA OF DAILY ACTIONS

Praying for the Three Yogas of Sleeping, Rising, and Experiencing Nectar

This is expressed in the dedication prayer, which states:

> By properly protecting the vows and commitments I received
> At that time as I would my eyeballs, as well as
> The yogas of sleeping, rising, and experiencing nectar,
> May my three doors delight in the three joys.

Furthermore, the Foremost Great Being [Tsongkhapa (1357–1419)] stated:

> The basis of accomplishing the two types of attainment is
> [Maintaining] pure vows and commitments.

Although you may not practice after obtaining an empowerment, if your general vows and commitments—and the root downfalls in particular—remain undefiled, you will not go to the lower realms even if you are pushed. At the very least, you will accomplish supreme attainments within sixteen lifetimes. Vibhuti[14] stated:

> Although you may not meditate, if you don't incur a downfall,
> You will accomplish purity within sixteen lives.

It has been taught that after obtaining empowerment, if your vows and commitments are not safeguarded purely, it will be like discarding a stone used for wiping your ass, and although you may subsequently claim that you are a practitioner of the two stages, it will be nothing more than a means of traversing to Vajra Hell. For that reason, the tantras and texts of the mahasiddhas state that when you receive a completely pure empowerment, the basis for accomplishing the two common and supreme attainments is properly protecting the commitments and vows

---

14. See Cyrus Stearns, "The Life and Tibetan Legacy of the Indian Mahapandita Vibhuticandra," *Journal of the International Association of Buddhist Studies* 19, no. 1 (1996):121–171.

that you received and promised to keep in the presence of the guru-deity. Once you discover complete uncontrived certainty concerning these points, you will protect them with the same care as you would your eyes. Undertaking your practice on that basis, you should also practice the yoga of the generation stage to primarily accomplish outer Dakini Land, and the yoga of the completion stage to primarily accomplish inner Dakini Land. Arya Nagarjuna stated:

> Those wishing for the completion stage
> Abide perfectly in the generation stage.
> This method is like a staircase
> Leading to complete enlightenment.

Initially you should train in the generation stage. Je Sachen [Kunga Nyingpo] stated the same when he proclaimed:

> Sleeping, rising, and experiencing nectar,
> The immeasurables, the guru, and generating oneself as
>   the deity,
> The yoga of purifying migrators,
> Being blessed by heroes and heroines,
> The verbal and mental recitation as one,
> The yoga of inconceivability,
> The yoga of daily actions—
> Thus, these are the eleven yogas.

The Yoga of Sleeping

Although this is technically classified among the yoga of daily actions, the reason we initiate our practice at this point is that rising must necessarily precede meditation on the other yogas, and prior to that you must sleep; therefore we begin in this way. Moreover, Mahasiddha Luipa stated:

> During the day, the Bhagavan vajra-holder;
> At night, the yoginis—so it is explained.

Night is the time to practice the yoga of sleeping. From among appearance and emptiness, that is the time of emptiness, and among method and wisdom, that is the time of wisdom. In general, the primary subject matter of Mother Tantra is the means of accomplishing the clear light as the factor of wisdom on the side of emptiness; therefore, if we initially undertake our practice at that time, it will be a quintessential point of auspiciousness for quickly generating that exalted wisdom in our mental continuum. The *Vajradaka* [*Tantra*] states:

> All the girls of this land
> Bestow attainments on practitioners;
> They always move about at night,
> They always assemble at night,
> They bestow the great attainment
> Of Dakini Land, so difficult to find.

Thus this is stating that the external goddesses always assemble and move about at night as dakinis, so if we initially commence our practice at that time, it becomes an essential feature that allows us to easily accomplish attainments of Dakini Land. If a person is *not* fond of elaborated practices or has a strong inclination toward emptiness, he [or she] should direct his [or her] efforts toward the completion stage, and when it is time to go to sleep should melt the world and its beings into light according to the common [yoga of] inconceivability, up to the point where only the nada remains, and then place the mind single-pointedly within the state of bliss and emptiness. This is the [yoga of] sleeping as commonly presented in the texts of highest yoga tantra, and is explained as an excellent and powerful means of apprehending the clear light of sleep. It has a qualitative similarity to the basis of purification as the disappearance of the worldly environment and the death of living beings as its inhabitants. For an ordinary being, the object of purification is ordinary sleep, and through the yoga of sleeping, it [i.e., ordinary sleep] is transformed into bliss and emptiness. Therefore it is extremely beneficial to mix the truth body of sleeping at the time of the path, and [this] is the agent ripening your roots of virtue in order to accomplish example [clear light] and meaning clear light, which in turn accomplishes the truth body as the result of purification.

Furthermore, if a person *is* fond of elaborative practices, he [or she] should direct his [or her] efforts toward the generation stage. Regarding this, you should visualize your dwelling as the double-tetrahedron phenomena source, inside of which is a lion throne, lotus, and sun-seat, upon which you appear clearly as the Venerable Mother without the ornaments or hand implements, with your head facing the northern petal where your root guru sits upon a sun- and moon-seat in the form of Hero Vajradharma facing west. You are lying down on your right side, with your right hand under your right cheek and your left hand upon your left thigh. Your legs can be either straight or bent as you sleep in the lion posture. Everything is the nature of radiant light. You should visualize this each time you awaken from your sleep.

Although the previous literary commentaries state that the guru is upon a lion throne, the oral instructions state that there are only sun- and moon-seats—which is easier to put into practice.

The Yoga of Rising

If the night is composed of eighteen sections; the time to rise is at dawn, during the five sections that occur once the thirteen previous sections have passed. Imagine that you are awoken from sleep by the heroes and dakinis of Dakini Land, with the sound of damarus and the three-OM mantra as they abide in space. If you slept according to the first system, you arise from within the state of bliss and emptiness in the aspect of the Venerable Mother, with ornaments but without hand implements, just as a fish leaps from water. If you practice according to the second system, you clarify your pure appearances and conceptions, and due to your faith and devotion for your guru, he [or she] transforms into a red orb of light the size of a bird's egg—and coming to rest on the crown of your head, dissolves into your mind as the syllable BAM at your heart, which radiates rays of light. This fills the inside of your body, purifying all your sickness, harm from spirits, negative karma, and obscurations, so that not even a fragment of them remains. Imagine that you develop the exalted wisdom of bliss and emptiness, whereby you become an even more glorious and radiant version of the Venerable Mother than you were previously.

The Yoga of Experiencing Nectar

You should practice this at the beginning of every session; therefore, as you undertake your session, you should place a nectar pill in the palm of your right hand, or, alternatively—if you have a skull cup for the inner offering—you can place one [nectar pill] in it and hold it so that the forehead is facing you. If you don't have one, you can also just imagine one, and as you recite OM AH HUM, draw the shape of a three-pointed phenomena source going counterclockwise in the palm of your right hand with the thumb and ring-finger of your left hand, so that the point is facing you. Extract the essence of the nectar from the center as the nature of bliss and emptiness, and taste it by placing it on your tongue, whereby your body is filled with nectar. Those luminous nectars dissolve into the syllable BAM at your heart, which is the mind of the Venerable Mother, who is the nature of all the buddhas and inseparable from your own mind. Imagining this causes you to generate the realization of bliss and emptiness and remain in a state of meditative stabilization for a short while. For practitioners of the Sakya tradition, the [yogas of sleeping, rising, and experiencing nectar] are called "the three joys." Je [Tsongkhapa] Father and Sons call them the "yoga of the three purifications," which other than some minor differences don't have any special difference in meaning and are nothing more than a means of identification. I have not composed more than this brief presentation for fear of being too verbose, and [because of] the fact that it is clear throughout the manuscript.

Thus you are praying, "Within the context of properly protecting my vows and commitments, may I purify all the faults, transgressions, and impurities of my three doors of body, speech, and mind through the yogas of sleeping, rising, and experiencing nectar, whereby they are revealed as the natural display of the three joys of body, speech, and mind, or, in other words, 'the three purifications.'"

Praying for the Yogas of the Immeasurables and the Guru

This is expressed in the dedication prayer, which states:

> Relying upon the nondeceptive objects of refuge as my
> crown-jewel,
> With the great purpose of mother sentient beings dwelling in my
> heart,
> And cleansing the stains of my transgressions with the nectar of
> Vajrasattva,
> May I be nurtured by the compassionate Venerable Guru.

The teachings also refer to these as "the four uncommon preliminaries." Furthermore, the guide of going for refuge functions to distinguish one from those engaged in the mistaken paths of non-Buddhists. The guide of generating bodhichitta functions to distinguish one from the lesser paths of shravakas and pratyekabuddhas. The guide of meditation and recitation of Vajrasattva functions to purify negative karma and obscurations. And the guide of guru yoga functions as the gateway to blessings. Therefore the first two are equivalent to the four immeasurables. To generate uncontrived bodhichitta that wishes to attain the state of enlightenment for the welfare of all living beings, you must precede it with the **four immeasurables** that think, "How I wish that all living beings, including enemies, friends, and strangers, could be free from attachment and anger for loved ones and strangers, and that they might be endowed with happiness; may they be free from suffering and never be separated from happiness." According to the assertion of [Drogon Chogyal] Phagpa Rinpoche [1235–1280], these two precede each other as cause and effect, whereby the aforementioned thoughts function as the cause of the four immeasurables, and as a result of this intention, bodhichitta emerges. Furthermore, it is asserted by Naropa and [Sachen Kunga Nyingpo] that once you have incorporated the four immeasurables within the mind of enlightenment, bodhichitta and the four immeasurables become one entity. Although this is in accordance with later [commentaries], it is not clearly explained in the former texts how to incorporate the four immeasurables within the mind of enlightenment. According to the manuscript of the Omniscient [Ngulchu] Dharmabhadra Palsangpo, this accords with the intention of the Foremost Great Being [Tsongkhapa].

With respect to **going for refuge**, it is taught to be the support of all vows; therefore going for refuge precedes bodhichitta. For that reason, you must initially visualize the objects that function as your basis of going for refuge, for which there are extensive, middling, and concise versions. The concise system is called "the all-encompassing jewel," for which Guru-Vajradharma functions as the sole object of refuge. For the middling system, you visualize the supporting and supported mandalas of the sixty-two deities of Heruka. For the extensive system, you visualize the Guru-Chakrasamvara Father and Mother surrounded by the Three Jewels. Therefore, this sadhana composed by my Foremost Guru [Ngulchu Dharmabhadra] is in accordance with the intention of the retreat manual of Changkya Rolpai Dorje. In that retreat manual it is the intention that there is no celestial mansion, which makes it easier to practice, yet it still utilizes the extensive system for the objects of refuge when it states, "In the space before me…." I have also presented the meaning of this dedication prayer from the perspective of his [i.e., Dharmabhadra's] sadhana.

Furthermore, without any ordinary appearances or conceptions, imagine that the ground is composed of lapis lazuli, upon which is a golden pattern directly before you, upon which is a precious throne upheld by eight lions. Its elevation is such that the heart of the principal [deity] is at your eye-level. It is [an] extremely vast and expansive [throne], upon which is a four-petaled lotus that is equal to the expanse [of the throne itself]. Its petals are green, its corolla is gold, and its rim is blue. In the center of that is [another] variegated lotus, with a lotus and moon, upon which is Guru-Chakrasamvara, with four faces [and] twelve arms, together with the Mother standing on Bhairava and Kalarati. Upon the corolla are the lineage gurus in the aspect of Hero Vajradharma. On the front petal is Vajrayogini, together with the tantric buddhas of the four classes of tantra. On the right petal is Buddha Shakyamuni with sutra buddhas, such as the thousand buddhas [of the fortunate eon]. On the back petal are the Dharma scriptures. On the left petal is Venerable

Manjushri, with the sutric Sangha as bodhisattvas, shravakas, and pratyekabuddhas, as well the tantric Sangha as heroes and dakinis. Upon
the rim are the various types of Sangha of sutra and tantra as Dharma
protectors, each appearing in his [or her] uncommon aspect.

Recite the lines "I and all migrating beings...."[15] This reveals that you
need to contemplate what exactly it is that you and all living beings are
relying upon as the causes of going for refuge and the times when you go
for refuge. Regarding the actual act of going for refuge, you recite, "Go
for refuge to the glorious guru...," and recite these four lines three times
and so forth. Furthermore, place your hopes in them from the depths
of your heart by contemplating, "You are the nondeceptive sources of
refuge" while possessing the two causes, and continue with, "Whatever
arises, whether happiness or suffering, you know what's best." Imagine,
"May I be capable of continuously relying upon the Three Jewels as the
source of refuge throughout all times, without any deception whatsoever, and hold them as my wish-fulfilling crown ornament until I attain
enlightenment." Refuge is the immeasurable preliminary.

With respect to **generating bodhichitta**, recite the verse that
states, "Once I attain the state of a perfectly complete buddha..." three
times or more, which, together with seeking refuge, causes a stream of
purifying nectar to descend. This is a means of utilizing the oral instructions for the resultant path, for generating bodhichitta incorporating
the objects of refuge. Furthermore, you can recite [additional prayers,
such as], "For the welfare of all mother living beings...." [Either way,]
develop a heartfelt determination to work for the welfare of others by
contemplating, "I alone shall accomplish the great aim of dispelling the
suffering and accomplishing everlasting happiness for all my mother living beings, who have cared for me with kindness since beginningless
time." Moreover, aspiring bodhichitta is striving for enlightenment with
the thought, "For that purpose, I shall attain enlightenment." Engaging
bodhichitta is the thought, "However, enlightenment cannot be attained
without causes and without conditions; therefore I shall engage in the
deeds of a bodhisattva in general, and in particular properly practice the

15. Throughout this text, the extractions from the sadhana are presented in the way they appear
in Pabongkha Dechen Nyingpo, *The Extremely Secret Dakini of Naropa: Vajrayogini Practice and
Commentary*, translated by David Gonsalez (Snow Lion, 2011).

liberating paths of Vajrayogini's generation and completion stages." This is the generation of bodhichitta and the actual yoga of the immeasurables.

Vajrasattva Meditation and Recitation

Although, according to the intention of the teachings presented in Changkya [Rolpai Dorje]'s text, this [Vajrasattva meditation] should be done in accordance with Heruka, according to the intention of the practice tradition, when it comes to the actual presentation in the sadhana, it is quite concise and not at all extensive, which is clear in Je Taranatha's [1575–1634] exhaustive commentary *Tsembu*.[16]

Generally, in Father Tantra, once you generate the Father and Mother adorned with both ornaments and garments, you recite the hundred-syllable mantra of Vajrasattva. Yet in Mother Tantra, the Father is adorned with six mudras and the Mother with five, while the Father holds a vajra and bell and the Mother holds a curved knife and skull cup and you recite the hundred-syllable mantra of Heruka.[17] However, in the Father Tantra of [Vajra-]Bhairava, it is explained that the Mother holds a curved knife and skull cup; therefore we shouldn't maintain that there is absolutely one fixed position. Thus as you recite, "A stream of nectar descends from Vajrasattva...," you should visualize Vajrasattva Father and Mother upon a lotus and moon seat on the crown of your head, with a syllable HUM upon a moon at his heart, surrounded by the white hundred-syllable mantra of Heruka, which is written in Tibetan block letters that are standing upright and facing inward while circling counterclockwise. Once you visualize this, you recite the mantra twenty-one times or more, whereby a stream of white nectar descends from [the mantra], during which you are supplicating, "May this have the capacity to cleanse all the negative karma, obscurations, faults, and downfalls I have accumulated with my three doors, without even the slightest bit remaining," which constitutes the meditation and recitation of Vajrasattva.

---

16. Tib. *tShems bu dmar khrid*. "*Tsembu*" means "to sew" or "to stitch two things together."
17. This is the Heruka-Vajrasattva mantra that begins "OM VAJRA HERUKA SAMAYA..."

HERO VAJRADHARMA

Guru Yoga

Recite the section that states "In the space before me…" up to "whereby his mind and mine become inseparably mixed." Moreover, although some [systems] explain the common meditation where your root guru is visualized as Hero Vajradharma, whereas another uncommon explanation states that he should be visualized as Buddha Vajradharma holding a vajra and bell, the text of my Venerable Guru [Ngulchu Dharmabhadra] is in accordance with the intention of Changkya [Rolpai Dorje] Rinpoche, which states that he is visualized as Hero Vajradharma. The idiom [is that] "there are three oral instructions for explaining 'free from duality.'" The equivalent term for "free from duality"[18] is "avadhuti,"[19] and means "abandoning duality" or "entering the [state] free from duality." Therefore, there are three primary channels in the body, namely, the central, right, and left. The right "roma" channel contains the wind of the "apprehender," and the left "kyangma" channel contains the wind of the "apprehended." To be free from the duality of the movement of these two [conceptions], the winds are halted, after which they enter, abide in, and dissolve into the central channel. During the explanation of the "great central channel" common to the Father and Mother, you visualize your root guru appearing in the aspect of Buddha Vajradharma, holding a vajra and bell and adorned with bone and jeweled ornaments.

During the explanation of the "lesser central channel" uncommon to the Mother, you visualize your guru in the aspect of Hero Vajradharma that is clearly set forth in [Changkya Rolpai Dorje's] text, which explains them using the phrase "common and uncommon." It is not as though they are somehow separate because in terms of nature they are equal, in that they are both completely enlightened beings with all the good qualities of abandonment and realization, and by relying upon them both you will accomplish realizations; therefore there is nothing special distinguishing them. Not only that, but if you mediate on the aspect of Vajradharma, since he is the nature of the vajra-speech [of all enlightened beings], it has the benefit of creating an auspicious condition for your mental continuum to be subdued by your guru. Ngawang Nyida Zangpo's[20] commentary on the eleven yogas states, "Meditating on Hero Vajradharma is uncommon to this practice. Holding a vajra and bell [as Guru Vajradharma] is common with Heruka." Jampa Chölek's[21] sadhana also states, "Visualize your root guru in the aspect of Venerable Vajradharma. Although some

---

18. Tib. *gnyis bral.*
19. "Avadhuti" is a Sanskrit term used in lieu of the term "central channel."
20. Ngawang Nyida Zangpo was an important Shangpa Kagyu Lama born in the sixteenth century.
21. Jampa Chölek was a Sakya lama whose dates are unknown to the Tibetan Buddhist Research Center. However, one of his teachers, sangs rgyas dpal bzang, was born in the fifteenth century.

people visualize Vajradharma holding a vajra and bell, that is done during the common presentation; therefore you should meditate on him in accordance with the uncommon practice tradition. Meditating on the aspect of Vajradharma creates an auspicious condition for bestowing the attainments of speech." Moreover, Je [Tuken] Losang Chökyi Nyima [1737–1802] stated that this has outer, inner, and secret aspects. Outwardly he is Hero Vajradharma, inwardly he is Buddha Vajradharma, and secretly he embraces the Mother Varahi. Meditating on the guru in this way comes from the guru's own oral instruction and is his own oral lineage, which I have not seen explained in any other texts. Nevertheless, the Father's katvanga symbolizes the Mother, and the Mother's katvanga symbolizes the Father; therefore in this practice there is no special distinction between Hero Vajradharma holding a katvanga and [Hero Vajradharma] embracing the Mother.

The phrase "the three practice traditions while explaining 'free from duality' in general" is in reference to generating the guru, dissolving the guru, and the uncommon yoga of inconceivability. There is also a system for explaining those three in relation to the instructions on the [state that is] "free from duality" of the completion stage. You may wonder whether perhaps the system of the three practice traditions has a different meaning during the [completion stage]. If you fabricate such thoughts, you should know that the practice [of the state that is free from duality] during the completion stage is the famous uncommon yoga of inconceivability. Regarding the famous uncommon yoga of inconceivability, it is primarily for accomplishing outer Dakini Land, as are the practices of the langali[ya] stem and so forth, which are practiced in conjunction with the generation stage; therefore they are not at all easy for ignorant beings such as myself to explain.

Moreover, during the practice of visualizing the concise objects of refuge as well as during the concise self-generation in accordance with the visualizations set forth in my own guru's retreat manual, you visualize your root guru as Hero Vajradharma alone; and that is called "the all-encompassing jewel" as the way of embodying all objects of refuge. The previous manuals state that all the gurus' mental continua have coalesced into a single mind stream; therefore [Hero Vajradharma] embodies all gurus. His five aggregates are the nature of the [five] buddha families;

therefore he is the Buddha jewel. His mental continuum is the Dharma with all good qualities of scripture and realization. The Sangha dwell in his outer and inner sources[22] and are the nature of bodhisattvas appearing as dakinis, guardians of the Dharma, and oath-bound protectors who are devout followers of the teachings; therefore the teachings present this system in which [the guru's] nature embodies all three objects of refuge. According to the manuscript of my Venerable Guru [Ngulchu Dharmabhadra], it is clear that he also asserts this system of embodying the three objects of refuge, and in dependence upon this you incorporate the objects of refuge; therefore it is obvious that his way of teaching is absolutely perfect and has a completely valid source.

Kusali Tsok

Moreover, at this point you offer your body, which the Nyingmas call "kusulu," which means "uncontrived ease,"[23] whereas those of the New Translation schools, such as Sachen [Kunga Nyingpo] and so forth, call it "kusali," which means "engaging in virtue." Although it is stated that the former is incorrect, my Venerable Guru [Ngulchu Dharmabhadra] said that they are both correct. The term "three perceptions" refers to eating and drinking, sleeping, and defecating, and is in reference to the fact that they seem to be unwholesome people who never do anything other than these three. In this instance as well, such persons never make an outward display of their scholarship or spiritual attainments. They don't engage in recitations, offerings, and so forth but instead spend day and night lying in bed while internally their minds are dwelling within a state of single-pointed absorption on the exalted wisdom of inseparable bliss and emptiness. While in this state they transform their bodies into nectar and offer it to the higher guests, practice generosity by sending it forth to the lower guests and so forth, and without making an outward display they easily accumulate a great store of merit. For that reason they are called "kusulu," or "uncontrived ease," which is designated by considering their external mode of appearance. The term "kusali," or

22. Tib. *skye mched*.
23. Tib. *ma bcos lhug pa*.

"endowed with virtue," is designated by considering their inner state of mind.

Mandala Offering

It is said that a mandala is an offering of attainment. If you are using it to accumulate a count [for a preliminary guide], you begin by offering one thirty-seven-heap mandala and then collecting a count using the seven-heap mandala, after which you end by offering one twenty-three-heap mandala. It is clear in the texts of the lineage that you offer one thirty-seven-heap mandala, and while you are offering the outer and inner objects of desire, you also offer the objects that generate attachment and so forth, which is most appropriate in the practice of action tantra. Regarding the actual practice, you recite "I offer the objects that produce my attachment, anger, and ignorance...," during which, if you visualize the pleasing objects that produce attachment, the displeasing objects that produce anger, and the various other objects that produce ignorance, and without any concern you set them upon the mandala as mental objects while supplicating the pacification of your attachment and anger, it is most excellent. With that in mind, recite "Venerable guru...," which is an offering of worship for your Venerable Root Guru as Hero Vajradharma and so forth in general; and in particular, once you present the kusali tsok as a preliminary accumulation of merit, you make a single-pointed request whereby you receive the blessing of the four empowerments, and while remaining within that state, you absorb [the guru] into you. Through this, your mind becomes inseparable in nature [from his or hers], and from this perspective you mix your mind and his [or hers] together as one. In this way you are praying, "May I be cared for by his [or her] great compassion until I attain enlightenment."

Praying for the Yoga of Self-Generation as the Deity has two sections:

1) PRAYING TO IDENTIFY THE ULTIMATE BASIS OF
   PURIFICATION AND SUBJUGATING THE DAKINIS
2) PRAYING FOR THE ACTUAL SELF-GENERATION AS
   THE DEITY

Praying to Identify the Ultimate Basis of Purification and Subjugating the Dakinis

This is expressed in the dedication prayer, which states:

> The outer yogini is the ravishing Mother of the Conquerors,
> The supreme inner Vajra Queen is the letter BAM,
> The secret dakini is clarity and emptiness of the nature of mind;
> May I delightfully partake in seeing their true identity.

Moreover, this is saying, "In dependence upon the gaining mastery over the dakinis dwelling in the three places, may I identify the ultimate basis of purification and realize their mode of manifestation from within the state of receiving the blessings of the simultaneously born yogini." There are three attributes for the basis of purification, namely, the 1) vast, 2) profound, and 3) ultimate basis of purification. From among these, the topic being covered here is the ultimate. Regarding this, it is the essential subject matter of all the systems of highest yoga Mantra, which are of one opinion in that the extremely subtle wind-and-mind that abides within the indestructible drop at the heart is the root of everything within samsara and nirvana and is the subtle basis for imputing the person. Yet taking this matter even further, during the practice of Vajrayogini's tantra, the teachings explicitly reveal the means of accomplishing the clear light within the context of wisdom, where emptiness functions as a cause of a similar type for accomplishing the mind of a conqueror as the truth body, through penetrating suchness by way of mahamudra as the simultaneously born exalted wisdom and its inseparability with empti- ness. However, it does not explicitly teach the means of accomplishing the illusory body as a factor of method on the side of appearances. It is not, however, stating that the wind as the basis of purification has an opposing characteristic, but explains the characteristics of the mind. For that reason, during this practice the teachings state, "The ultimate basis of purification is your mind of simultaneously born exalted wisdom that is free from all extremes of verbal designations." Regarding this, the extremely subtle mind of the all-empty clear light is your innate mind, or, in other words, your "primordial" mind. Regarding this, there is the basis at the time of death, as well as when the winds dissolve into the central channel through the force of meditating on the path and you experience a direct realization in which the nature of that experience is free from all extremes of conceptual elaboration. This is similar to a direct realization of emptiness in which that pure empty state is the appearing object. However, that lasts for only an instant in the minds of all [ordinary beings]; therefore they are unable to dwell within that state for a protracted period of time.

From the context of its intrinsic nature, it [i.e., your innate mind] has existed since beginningless time until the present and is not altered in the slightest by virtue and nonvirtue, and even once you attain its [realization], its [nature] does not change and is said to be naturally pure, like the rays of the sun. Therefore it is also improper to think that the primordial mind is affected by the stains of attachment and so forth, and that they [i.e., the primordial mind and the stains of attachment] abide together as a single [entity]. Regarding the fact that you do not perceive [the primordial mind] directly although it is presently residing within you, once it is obscured by the stains of attachment and so forth, it is imperceptible, and although you may directly perceive the natural state of the primordial mind, you are incapable of expressing its exact mode of existence.

The *Hevajra [Tantra]* states:

> Others cannot express the innate mind
> And they cannot find it anywhere.

[Mahasiddha] Saraha proclaimed:

> There is no one who can characterize the nature of the primordial mind.

And:

> Although words cannot express the nature of the primordial mind,

You perceive it through the oral instructions of the master.

For that reason, from among the outer, inner, and secret yoginis, the emptiness and clarity of your innate mind is the secret dakini, and through the dependent relationship of that, the right and left channels glide into the central channel at the navel, forming a triangle in the shape of the syllable EH, and within it the two red elements glow, and the three glowing together form the shape of a short-AH, which in this system is called "tilaka" (or drop), while their roundness forms the shape of a syllable VAM,[24] which is the inner yogini. With respect to abiding externally in Akanishta [Pure Land], this is the best of the outer yoginis and is the "simultaneously born dakini." Those that abide in the twenty-four holy places of this world and so forth are the field-born dakinis and are middling [yoginis]. Those who have attained realizations of the generation stage and higher by training in the common path and uncommon stages of the path are the mantra-born yoginis and are lesser [yoginis]. Moreover, while the holy guru is giving the blessings of this tradition, it is done by way of identifying the generation of the inner yogini, absorption of the outer yogini, and visualizing the secret dakini. Through the continuous practice of identifying, through either the generation or completion stage, other than cultivating that which was introduced during the empowerment there is no need to practice anything else. Therefore in this practice, during the generation and completion stages you repeatedly meditate on that which was introduced during the blessing [empowerment]; and with this serving as the inner condition, you first realize the mantra-born [yogini], then sequentially master the stage of the field-born dakini. Thus you are praying, "By means of such a practice, may I directly perceive the true identity of the perfect display of the three outer yoginis that manifest for the benefit of their disciple, and delightfully partake in single-pointed absorption."

With the central channel path of the completion stage as the inner condition, you engage in meditation once you penetrate the vital points of the channel wheel of the central channel. Having subjugated the daki-

---

24. In Tibetan this is presented as a syllable BAM.

nis as the outer condition for a karma mudra,[25] they enter into embrace
in dependence upon which all the winds enter, abide in, and dissolve
into their central channel and the downward-voiding wind leaves the
bhaga[26] of the mudra like a stiff waft of incense and enters the pathway
of your central channel. Through this, your downward-voiding wind is
reversed and drawn upward, after which the red element at your navel
as the drop of Varahi—appearing in the aspect of a red syllable BAM
that is the supreme inner Vajra Queen, which is the nature of blazing
fire—blazes upward and melts the white element at the crown of your
head that is the nature of Heruka. These meet and coalesce as the red
and white elements at your heart. Thus you are saying, "May I delightfully partake of the experience of perceiving their true nature." Thus,
through the meeting and coalescing of the red and white elements, you
sequentially induce the four joys, and you meditate by conjoining bliss
and emptiness during the general and particular simultaneously born
[bliss]. In this way you are praying, "May I delightfully partake of bliss and
emptiness once the coarse dualistic appearances of appearance, increase,
and near-attainment have dissipated by directly perceiving the emptiness
and clarity of the simultaneously born exalted wisdom of the primordial
mind as the all-empty clear light and perceive the true identity of the
Secret Mother of Dakini Land exactly as it occurs at the time of the
base." Through this, you are praying for blessings to accomplish that.

Nevertheless, the very innate mind of clear light does not counteract
self-grasping and its actual mode of apprehension, which is the root of
samsara; therefore that alone will not liberate you from samsara. Protector Nagarjuna proclaimed:

> Whoever does not understand emptiness
> Will most certainly not be liberated.
> The six types of migrating beings are imprisoned in existence
> As their ignorance perpetuates samsara.

25. In previous texts I have translated this as "action mudra," but use "karma mudra" here since
the Tibetan term *las* is a translation of the Sanskrit word "karma," which is intended to indicate
that such a consort is a human being born through the force of karma.
26. "Bhaga" is a Sanskrit word used honorifically in tantric texts to refer to the vagina of a
karma mudra. Another term often used is "secret lotus," or simply "lotus."

The teachings also state that there is no difference in the emptiness presented in either sutra or tantra. For that reason, if you haven't come to absolute certainty about your understanding of the emptiness of no-self, you will not be liberated from samsara. And if the mind with that understanding is not brought together with the previous explanation about the exalted wisdom of simultaneously born great bliss, it will not have the essential feature of highest yoga tantra; therefore both [emptiness and the blissful mind of clear light] are needed.

Saraha proclaimed:

> You will not attain the supreme path when
> You abide in emptiness without compassion.
>
> Yet if you only meditate on compassion, you
> Will also not attain liberation from this abode of samsara.
>
> Whoever develops their capacity for both
> Will dwell neither in nirvana nor samsara.

Thus, utilizing the secret yogini as the exalted wisdom of simultaneously born great bliss is the way and means of actualizing the generic image of the true nature of reality through which the innate example—or, in other words, example clear light—dawns, and through familiarizing yourself with that, the impure illusory body arises as the actual [deity] body. Moreover, through dwelling in the clear light, you directly realize the true nature of reality through the simultaneously born exalted wisdom, and [thereby] realize meaning clear light. Next, you will sequentially actualize the union of learning and no-more-learning and attain the state of Vajrayogini. For that reason, if you are able to attract and find the outer yogini in general, and field-born and simultaneously born yoginis in particular, you will quickly complete the entire path. This path of Chakrasamvara Father and Mother has many such special corresponding methods of dependent relationship, and because it possesses such a path, it is far superior to other practices.

Praying for the Actual Self-Generation as the Deity

This is expressed in the dedication prayer, which states:

> May I complete the yoga of generating myself as the deity,
> The supreme ripening agent for developing realizations of the
>   path and result,
> As the wondrous method of bringing the basis of purification—
> Death, the intermediate state, and rebirth—into the path of the
>   three bodies.

Regarding this, this is covered in the sadhana in the section that begins "The very letter BAM increases in size…" and continues up to "I stand in the center of a blazing fire of exalted wisdom." Furthermore, with respect to what is the basis of purification, it is death, the intermediate state, and rebirth. Moreover, you are not training in death, the intermediate state, and rebirth for other migrating beings, for other places of rebirth, for other worlds, or for a person who is separate from your own mental continuum. The principal trainee of highest yoga Mantra is a womb-born human being endowed with the six elements,[27] born in this world that is the basis for accomplishing enlightenment in one life, with extremely sharp faculties, who is capable of utilizing bliss on the path. Beings in the two higher realms, the four higher gods of the desire realm, and hell beings do not have the bliss of sexual union. The gods of the Realm of the Thirty-Three and those in abodes of the Four Great Kings do not even have the mere bliss of briefly uniting the winds by way of the channels and the red and white elements; therefore this is also not the bliss of their sexual contact. Although hungry ghosts and animals do experience the bliss of sexual contact, they are greatly obscured by their karma and are of extremely dull faculties; therefore they are incapable of utilizing bliss on the path. Therefore, [all] these are not suitable to be the principal trainees of highest yoga Mantra. Regarding the phrase,

---

27. The six inner elements are earth, water, fire, winds, channels, and drops.

"Although the humans in the three other world systems[28] also have enjoyments," they have great enjoyments, and [moreover,] the lengths of their lives, the qualities of their bodies, whether they are rich or poor, whether or not they are ill, and whether they have happiness or suffering are for the most part balanced; therefore their characteristics disqualify them from developing renunciation while other characteristics make compassion difficult, and although they have the bliss of sexual contact, they are of dull faculties; therefore they are incapable of undertaking the path.

The phrase "The karma of human beings in this world system" refers to the fact that [human beings in this world system] are capable of experiencing the ripening of karma in the later parts of their lives that they created in the earlier parts of their lives. Additionally, the length of their lives, the quality of their bodies, their status, their happiness and suffering, and so forth are unique, making it easy for them to develop renunciation and compassion. They are endowed with the six elements of earth, water, fire, winds, channels, and drops. They also have sharp faculties; therefore they are capable of utilizing the bliss from the union of their red and white elements on the path. Not only that, but they need a basis, path, and result that correspond to all circumstances, and other than our Teacher [Shakyamuni], who revealed the resultant supreme emanation body and engaged in the twelve deeds in the aspect of a womb-born human being endowed with the six elements, the other worlds and other places of rebirth do not have such a teacher. For these reasons the basis of purification is your forthcoming death, intermediate state, and rebirth that will occur in the future for yourself as a human-born practitioner of this world endowed with the six elements.

Regarding the means of purifying these, [the sadhana] states, "The very letter BAM increases in size...." At this point in the Sakya tradition, they don't do anything other than expand the syllable BAM outward. However, to once again retract it to the size of a small syllable BAM [as done in this tradition] has a very special attribute that functions as a profound ripening agent for the completion stage. Among the two sequential withdrawals during the completion stage—namely, holding the body

---

28. In ancient Buddhist cosmology, our world system consists of Mount Meru, which is surrounded by a great ocean, with four continents in the four cardinal directions, each with two subcontinents.

entirely and the stage of subsequent destruction[29]—this corresponds to the latter [stage of subsequent destruction]. In particular, during the completion stage, the rays of light and so forth that are projected outward are absolutely withdrawn once more back into the basis from which they were projected, and during the purification of negative karma and obscurations you also don't visualize [the impurities] being dispelled outward; therefore it is an extremely subtle point that you absolutely must not merely emanate outward from the syllable BAM and then just leave it. Moreover, after you have dissolved your guru [into yourself], your mind and your guru's mind of inseparable bliss and emptiness are one in nature as the syllable BAM, which becomes increasingly larger in size, pervading the mantra rosary and the phenomena source, your body, your homeland, the boundary of your country, the kingdom governed by the Chakravartin King, and so on, until all worlds and their beings equal to the extent of space become the nature of that single syllable BAM that is the nature of bliss and emptiness.

Next, the system of withdrawal is in accordance with [Heruka] Father teachings of Ghantapa's Five Deity [practice]; therefore it is once again sequentially withdrawn from the edges, and the syllable BAM becomes increasingly smaller until the earth element dissolves into the water element and there is the mirage-like appearance. When the body [of the BAM] dissolves into the head [of the BAM], the water element dissolves into the fire element and you experience the smoke-like appearance. As the head [of the BAM] dissolves into the crescent moon, the fire element dissolves into the wind element and you experience the inner sign of the fireflies-like appearance. When the crescent moon dissolves into the drop, the wind [element] dissolves into consciousness and you experience the blazing-candle-flame-like appearance. These are the four signs.

When the drop dissolves into the nada, the white bodhichitta that initially abides in the channel wheel at the crown flows downward within the central channel until it reaches the heart and you experience the first empty, called "the path of the white appearance." Next, the lower

29. During "the stage of subsequent destruction," the world and its beings melt into light and dissolve into you, and you subsequently dissolve into emptiness; during "holding the body entirely," the world and its beings are left intact, and only the body is sequentially dissolved into emptiness.

curve of the three-curved nada dissolves from below, during which the red element within the channel wheel at the navel—which is of the nature of fire—flows upward within the central channel to the heart, at which point you experience the second empty, called "the path of red increase." When the middle curve dissolves into the upper curve, the red and white elements encapsulate the indestructible drop within the center of the channel wheel at your heart and the red and white drops conjoin, and those two halves [form something similar to] a split pea, in the center of which is your extremely subtle wind-and-mind. Due to the upper and lower parts encapsulating it, you experience the third empty, called "the path of black near-attainment." During the beginnings of this encapsulation you still have mindfulness, but during the second half of the encapsulation you are without mindfulness and it is as though you lose consciousness; however, this is not a fault but a good quality because the degree to which you lose consciousness is the degree to which the forthcoming clear light will be stable and intense.

As the tip of the nada completely disappears into a state of emptiness, the upper and lower halves of the red and white elements that encapsulate the indestructible drop continue to move upward and downward; you actualize the natural radiance of your extremely subtle wind-and-mind, during which it is free from the three faults[30] of contamination; and the fourth empty, called "the all-empty clear light," dawns.

During the four empties in general and the fourth empty in particular, there is absolutely no appearance of the world and its beings as the appearing object; instead, there is a pristine vacuity. The object of experience is your own extremely subtle wind-and-mind, which has become the nature of great bliss, and its mode of apprehension is that all phenomena are mere imputations of your own mind, and other than this they don't have even an atom of inherent existence from their own side. Although this has not transcended a very subtle dualistic appearance between the subjective ascertaining consciousness and the objective emptiness, they [i.e., the extremely subtle subjective mind of clear light as the ascertaining factor and the objective emptiness as the object

30. The three faults are the dualistic appearances of the minds of white appearance, red increase, and black near-attainment.

ascertained] have become like water poured into water. Moreover, you don't think that you are merely an ordinary person but [realize] that [your mind experiencing great bliss] is the actual truth body of exalted wisdom as the actual mind of Vajrayogini, together with divine pride possessing the four essential features.[31] You don't sustain this for just a short while but practice **bringing death into the path as the truth body** for a protracted period of time.

Next, you set forth your intention to assume a form body for the welfare of living beings, imagine that your mind as the truth body appears abiding in space as the extremely subtle syllable BAM, and practice **bringing the intermediate state into the path as the enjoyment body.**

Visualize that below the syllable BAM are two stacked EH syllables, from which emerges a red double tetrahedron together with four joyswirls in the center of which, from AH, emerges a white moon with a red luster with a rosary of the three-OM mantra at its edge, which is red in color, standing upright, and written in Tibetan block letters that face inward. They are like an encircling rosary of rubies. When your mind as the syllable BAM sees the moon, it thinks, "I must assume a coarse emanation body for the welfare of others," and with this intention the syllable BAM enters into the center of the moon. In dependence upon light rays radiating and retracting from the moon, the syllable BAM, and the mantra rosary, the supporting protection circle and phenomena source—together with the supported body of the Venerable Mother—are generated simultaneously, and they establish a clear visualization in stages, which functions to develop your divine pride of being the resultant Venerable Vajrayogini. This is **bringing rebirth into the path of the emanation body**.

Although there are different systems asserting the way to arrange the three-OM mantra rosary, this [one] finds its ultimate source in Naropa's *Small Treatise*, which states, "Imagine the system of the mantra rosary reversed." The meaning of "reversed" is counterclockwise, which is clear

---

31. The four essential features are: 1) all conventional appearances have subsided, leaving a pure vacuity, 2) that vacuity is ascertained as the emptiness of inherent existence, 3) your mind is experiencing great bliss, and 4) you identity this as the truth body of Vajrayogini and establish it as your basis for imputing "I."

in a footnote of that text. That footnote was composed by Sachen [Kunga Nyingpo] and is clear in the "Teachings Received"[32] from the Supreme Conqueror the Fifth [Dalai Lama]. Moreover, it does not contradict the texts to arrange the mantra counterclockwise; therefore "reversed" has the same meaning as "counterclockwise." "Forward progression" or "not reversed from standard tradition" both have the same meaning as "clockwise." The way of reversing them comes from the eighth chapter of the *Heruka Root Tantra*, where it presents the mantra as: "HA SÖ PHAT HUM HUM YE NI NA WA VAJRA YE NE KI DA DHA BU WA SAR OM." Je [Tsongkhapa] addresses this topic of reversing the mantra head-on in [his commentary on the *Heruka Root Tantra* entitled] *A Clear Illumination of All Hidden Meaning*[33] when he proclaims, "When arranging the mantra, it should be set forth in reverse order as 'HA SÖ' and so on." In the [*Heruka Root*] *Tantra*[34] it is set forth that way to conceal its natural sequence. If we explain the mantra in its correct sequence, it would read "OM SARWA BUDDHA...."

For that reason, if you are writing one syllable, the reader would go from right to left when reading and inquire about the counterclockwise reverse sequence, and when it is read from left to right, he [or she] could inquire about the forward progression from right to left. Regarding this, the "Syllable Blessing"[35] of Muchen Sangye Palsang states, "Write the three-OM mantra with its heads facing outward, [beginning] in the front and going counterclockwise."

In reference to this, they are written in proper sequence and set forth as OM OM OM / SARWA / BUDDHA / DAKI / NI YE / VAJRA / WARNA / NI YE / VAJRA / BERO / TSA NI YE / HUM HUM HUM / PHAT PHAT PHAT / SÖHA /. Furthermore, it states that it would be best if they were written so that the OM is directly east, the DA to the north, the NA to the west, and the NI to the south. Simi-

---

32. Tib. *bsan yig*. This is a genre of material that lists the teachings received, given, and composed by a given lama.
33. Tib. *sBas don kun gsal*.
34. This means that the mantras were set forth in reverse order so that the uninitiated would be unable to properly pronounce them. A translation of the *Heruka Root Tantra* is available at: www.dechenlingpress.org.
35. Tib. *byin rlabs kyi yi ge*.

larly, Tsarchen [Losal Gyatso's] *Quick Path to Accomplishing Dakini Land*[36] states, "Arrange the three-OM mantra rosary counterclockwise, facing outward toward the perimeter, written so that it ends in front of the syllable BAM. Furthermore, after the three OMs is SARWA." He continues, "Do not reverse the sequence of the letters individually with the exception of SÖHA." And continues, "For this, the first syllable in the east is OM" and "if you arrange the syllable NI in the south, they will be equally dispersed." The rest of the teaching does not have any significant differences from the previous [explanation].

The *Quick Path to Accomplishing Dakini Land* states, "Arrange the mantra rosary counterclockwise on the rim of the moon, with the three OMs in front of the BAM. Next is SARWA BUDDHA DAKINIYE VAJRA WARNANIYE VAJRA BEROTZANIYE; continue with the letters reversed in groups of two, and then end with three HUMs, three PHATs, and SÖHA, so that the HA and OM meet up next to each other." Regarding the phrase "reversed in groups of two," [The Sakya lama] Panchen Ngawang Chödrak [1572–1641] states, "Moreover, the three OMs are in front of the BAM, and close to that is SARWA, reversed so that it reads WA SAR, which is next to BUDDHA, reversed to read DDHA BU. Next to that is KI DA, next to that is YE NI, next to that is VAJRA, next to that is NA WAR, next to that is YE NI, next to that is VAJRA, next to that is RO BE, next to that is YE NE TSA, next to that are the three HUMs and the three PHATs, next to that is SÖHA, which lines up perfectly to the root [i.e., first] OM." Although when SARWA is reversed it reads WA SAR, SARWA is written in its reverse order counterclockwise; therefore it has the same meaning.

Therefore, if you write out [the mantra] according the teachings in that text, whatever letter you have should meet up with the three OMs, which accords with the teachings set forth in the [*Heruka Root*] *Tantra*, which states that they are arranged in reverse order counterclockwise and that OM and HA meet up next to each other. Regarding the meaning of the statement [quoted above,] "Do not reverse sequence of the letters individually," this means do not reverse each one out separately. For instance, if you have a [left-facing] DA, do not write SAR DA [with

36. Tib. *mKha' spyod bsgrub pa'i nye lam.*

the DA facing to the right]; if you have a [right-facing] DA, do not write SAR DA [with the DA facing to the left]; if you have a [left-facing] NA, do not write SAR NA [with a right-facing NA], and so on. If you arrange them in that way, the OM will be directly to the east, the DA to the north, and NI to the south, and they will come out equally spaced, which is exactly what is intended. Those in the northeast have vowels, six in the northwest, six in the southwest, and seven in the southeast without vowels. If the last three are arranged as stacked, there will be nine in the southeast. If they are arranged in that way, we may ask about the PHA and T [of PHAT], which would put nine in the southeast.

Therefore, if we follow the latter system, directly to the south is OM, in the north is KI, in the west is VAJRA with the VA in the latter position, in the south is HUM, which if it is followed by BYA will definitely come out so that it is arranged equally. For this, some people say that each letter should not be written out separately, stating that this has a different meaning from "each one arranged counterclockwise," and that the intention is not that each of the two letters in the stacked letters is reversed but that they are set out counterclockwise.

Although this line of inquiry works for stacked letters such as BUD-DHA, SARWA, OM, and so on,[37] the HA [of SÖHA] and OM will not come out next to each other. Yet it is not appropriate if you assert that each letter in SÖHA [so that it reads SÖ and HA] is reversed and then arrange each of the remaining pairs of the mantra counterclockwise, because you will need to stack the letters and it is inappropriate to stack SÖHA because they need to be reversed, which is illogical.

The previous system of arranging them equally also works out so that they are extremely unequal in the northeast. There are seven in the northwest, four in the southwest, [and] eight in the southeast with vowels, [but] with nine and PHAT separated [in the northeast], you get twelve, which is so obvious that even a cattle herder could understand it, despite the fact that there are many that are unequally arranged—four, nine, and so forth. The Powerful Scholar and Siddha Tsarchen Father and Sons did not introduce such a mistaken system, which is like a blind

---

37. In Tibetan, these letters are compiled by stacking letters on top of each other, making them more syllables than letters.

man's cane, and such a thing could not exist even in a dream. For that reason, if you undertake an exhaustive, detailed examination of these with a fair mind, you will see that this line of inquiry about reversing each of the two letters is not the intention of Tsarchen Father and Sons.

Moreover, there is also a system of the syllable BAM reading the mantra rosary during recitation. In particular, although you read from right to left, you ignore the valid meaning of the letters in the three-OM mantra, just as an old dog mindlessly gobbles down a discarded hide, and therefore you don't strive to accomplish the meaning of the mantra, such as "the dakini of all the buddhas" and so forth,[38] which is the antithesis of the assertion of this tantra, of the Mahasiddha Tsarchen, and so forth, and [which also] completely contradicts the extracts from the mantra. If you utilize the way of arranging [the mantra] in the reverse counterclockwise order, you should arrange the mantra rosary counterclockwise in accordance with the Father [Heruka] and so forth. If, although you do everything just right, you still look for some new explanation that is somehow better than the well-known system of the past, you will be like someone who is blind himself even though he is supposed to be leading the blind, and [thus] utterly helpless, without any sense of direction.

Once you understand these reasons, you should follow the teachings in accordance with assertions of Je Takphu's commentary on the two stages entitled *A Staircase of Pure Lapis*,[39] which states that the stacked letters are reversed, after which it states, "Alternatively, it is also best if it is counterclockwise, in accordance with certain commentaries taught by the guru." Regarding the "guru," this is a reference to the mandala rituals of the Supreme Siddha Jamyang Depai Dorje and [Tuken] Losang Chökyi Nyima, which also state that each of the letters during the sindhura mandala of mind should not be reversed, but that it would be best if each letter were reversed in accordance with the general counterclockwise formula. Saying that this was taught by the lama means that it is in agreement with the lama's teachings, which in this case are in reference to both Je Takphu and Je Changkya Rolpai Dorje. For that reason, with respect to these Fathers and Sons, the definitive meaning [of the mantra]

---

38. This is the translation equivalent of SARWA BUDDHA DAKINIYE.

39. Tib. *Bai DU r-ya zhun ma'i them skas*; composed by the Fourth Takphu Rinpoche, blo bzang bstan pa'i rgyal mtshan.

is nondual with Glorious Heruka, and the interpretive meaning appears according to the disposition of the disciple who is discovered at the lotus feet of the qualified lama with boundless [qualities], who is like an ocean of oral instructions of sutra and tantra and who has perfected listening, contemplating, and meditating by coming to a proper understanding, induced through the path of reasoning examining the meaning of the sutras and tantras, and who has struck the gold of fearlessness and is nothing less than an incomparable great being endowed with scholarship and attainments. Therefore, their [i.e., qualified lamas'] teachings directly reveal what is correct while indirectly revealing what is incorrect. My own Foremost Lama [Ngulchu Dharmabhadra] also discovered absolute certainty induced through the boundless path of scripture and reasoning. According to his lucid manuscript, [what is described above is] the way to arrange the three-OM mantra rosary, and he correspondingly composed a brand new, unprecedented sindhura mandala. Therefore, by following the meaning of this, none of the [aforementioned] faults has found its way into [Ngulchu's sindhura mandala arrangement]. Nevertheless, since the previous beings [i.e., gurus] who assert these other systems are such great beings that merely hearing their names robs samsara of its torments, they must have had a special purpose in establishing their systems. Foolish and ignorant beings such as ourselves, who are not even soiled with the sweat of their good qualities, cannot do anything but prostrate and go for refuge to them from the depths of our hearts. Therefore, concerning this, there have been a few bad men of the past who are filled with nothing but jealousy and talk nonsense, and [who,] their manuscript being very brief, elaborate only slightly and therefore do very little toward dispelling the doubts of those upholding our tradition.

In that way, during the first stage [i.e., the generation stage], all three bases of purification are accomplished through the skillful and wondrous means of bringing death into the path as the truth body, the intermediate state into the enjoyment body, and rebirth into the emanation body, together with extremely powerful divine pride that thinks, "I have actually achieved [those three bodies]." Relying upon this extraordinary path functions as an agent ripening your roots of virtue to generate in your mental continuum the path of example [clear light] and meaning clear light, which during the second stage [i.e., the completion stage] occurs when the coarse and subtle winds all dissolve into the heart in dependence upon the inner and outer methods.[40] As a result of that, you directly realize the clear light of the truth body of no-more-learning, which functions to ripen your virtuous roots to accomplish the actual path of the pure and impure illusory bodies,[41] so that the moment you arise from that clear light, you arise in the form and shape [of your deity] separate from your old aggregates. As the ultimate result of that, you directly realize the resultant complete enjoyment body, which in turn functions to ripen your virtuous roots for the illusory body to assume a coarse emanation body. As a result of that, you gain the realization of the enjoyment body assuming a coarse emanation body. In that way, this is the supreme means of ripening your virtuous roots during the path to generate realizations of the resultant state. Thus you are praying, "May I perfect the yoga of mentally generating myself in the aspect of the supporting phenomena source and supported Venerable Mother."

Praying for the Yoga of Purifying Migrating Beings

This is expressed in the dedication prayer, which states:

> The worldly environment is the celestial mansion of the
>   letter EH,
> The sentient beings who inhabit them are the yoginis of the
>   syllable BAM;
> Through the concentration of the great bliss union [of EVAM],
> May whatever appears arise as pure appearances.

For that, the sadhana states "At my heart is a red phenomena source…" and continues up to "all transform into the body of Vajrayogini." For this, there are two bases of purification related to others. Regarding the first of these two, within your heart is a double tetrahedron similar to the

---

40. The outer method is relying upon a karma mudra (see note 25 above), and the inner method is either of the two concentrations called "holding the body entirely" and "the stage of subsequent destruction" (see note 29).
41. The impure illusory body arises from example clear light, and the pure illusory body arises from meaning clear light.

external celestial mansion, in the center of which is a moon mandala with a red syllable BAM in its center, facing forward. Surrounding that, beginning in front and going counterclockwise, is a circle of the three-OM mantra as a red mantra rosary, from which five-colored light rays radiate. On the tips of the white light rays are the assembly of deities of the body wheel; on the tips of the red light rays are those of the speech wheel; on the tips of the blue light rays are those of the mind wheel; on the tips of the yellow light rays are those of the great bliss wheel; and on the tips of the green light rays are those of the commitment wheel.[42] Or, if your mind is not very disciplined, you can just imagine the five-colored rays of light that radiate out from your hair pores. Imagine that, by merely being touched by these light rays, the faults of the environment—such as large rocks, pebbles, gravel, cliffs and ravines, and large abysses—are instantaneously purified, as are the faults of the beings therein, such as their negative karma, obscurations, attachments, and so forth.

Regarding the second [basis of] transformation, imagine that all environments appear as the phenomena source that is the nature of bliss and emptiness, and that all beings therein transform into the aspect of Vajrayogini. This process purifies your impure appearances and conceptions and completes a great collection of merit that is very similar to [the results of] the Mahayana practice of taking and giving (tonglen), except that its superiority far exceeds even that. It is taught that it has characteristics similar to those of the concentration called "the supreme conqueror of the mandala" found in other practices.[43]

In that way, all external worldly environments arise from the syllable EH as the celestial mansion in the aspect of a double-tetrahedron phenomena source, and all living beings therein arise from the syllable BAM as Vajrayogini. Thus you are praying, "May whatever worlds and their beings that appear all arise solely in the aspect of the supporting

---

42. This is in reference to the five wheels of the Chakrasamvara body mandala practice. The body mandala of Vajrayogini contains all the dakinis of the five wheels in a much simpler presentation.

43. For a detailed description of "the supreme conqueror of the mandala," see Ngulchu Dharmabhadra and the Fifth Ling Rinpoche, *The Roar of Thunder: Yamantaka Practice and Commentary*, available exclusively at www.dechenlingpress.org.

and supported [mandalas], through the force of such a concentration of bliss and emptiness as the union of EVAM."

Praying for the Yoga of Being Blessed by Heroes and Heroines

This is expressed in the dedication prayer, which states:

> Visualizing my inner channels as the thirty-seven deities,
> Dissolving all phenomena of samsara and nirvana into the nature
> Of the three messengers, and wearing the armor of the
>   mantra-syllables,
> May I never be disrupted by outer and inner interferences.

For this, the sadhana states, "If you wish, you should meditate on the body mandala at this point."[44] Although it states that it is up to you whether or not you do the meditation [on the body mandala], it is not included in the ritual; therefore if you wish to meditate [on the body mandala], you should follow the teachings on being blessed by heroes and heroines as presented in [Tsarchen's] *Quick Path to Accomplishing Dakini Land*. However, the teachings according to Tsarchen's own advice in the footnotes—as well as Je [Tsongkhapa] Rinpoche, Changkya Rolpai Dorje [Rinpoche], and so on—state that you should [in fact] meditate [on the body mandala] at this point. With respect to this, the sadhana states, "The red section within my heart..." and continues up to "standing on Bhairava and Kalarati with her right leg outstretched."[45] For this, there is the common presentation taken from other practices of Varahi's body mandala where [the body-mandala deities] are visualized at the outer tips of the channels, yet Naropa's practice of the Venerable Mother is in agreement with the uncommon Hearing Lineage, which visualizes them at the inner tips of the channels at the heart. From between these two systems, in this practice we follow the latter.

44. This appears in the older sadhanas but not in the sadhana compiled by Pabongkha Rinpoche.
45. Again, this is slightly different from the presentation in Pabongkha Rinpoche's sadhana. See Pabongkha Dechen Nyingpo, *The Extremely Secret Dakini of Naropa* (Snow Lion, 2011), pp. 291–92.

Furthermore, one option would be to not withdraw the syllable BAM and mantra rosary, whereby they become the substantial cause [of the body-mandala deities] and duplicates emerge from the channels and elements, or the channels and elements sequentially dissolve inward, whereby they function as the contributory cause and generate the thirty-seven deities. Alternatively, you can withdraw the syllable BAM and mantra rosary and then visualize the channels and elements that melt and transform into the five letters, namely, the short-AH, YA, RA, LA, and WA, as well as the syllables of the three-OM mantra, which are then generated as the thirty-seven deities. Whichever system you use, there is a moon mandala within the phenomena source at your heart upon which are the yoginis—the nature of your channels—standing upon Bhairava and Kalarati. [The yoginis] hold katvangas, which symbolize the heroes that are the nature of your channels. The thirty-two deities of the eight goddesses of the corners and doors, as well as twenty-four heroines of the body, speech, and mind wheels together with four Mothers of the great bliss wheel, are the thirty-seven deities and are the nature of the Principal Mother. You should think that these are the actual heroes and yoginis who reside in the thirty-seven places as the twenty-four holy places, the eight great charnel grounds, the four continents, and Mount Meru. Moreover, you should imagine that they are accomplished from a part of your body.

With respect to the actual blessing of the heroes and heroines, the sadhana states, "PHAIM! Light rays radiate from the letter BAM at my heart…" and continues up to "I am the nature of the yoga of the perfect purity of all phenomena." This is also called "mixing the three messengers" and means that once you invoke the wisdom beings before you, they are absorbed. Moreover, proclaim "PHAIM" as **mantra** together with the blazing **mudra**. And, with either the external yoginis or the body mandala, red light rays radiate from the syllable BAM at the heart of [either of the internal or external] Principal Mother—as well as the four yoginis—and leave between their eyebrows and go to the ten directions, invoking all the tathagatas as well as the simultaneously born, field-born, and mantra-born yoginis and so forth, together with all the gurus, personal deities, buddhas, bodhisattvas, heroes, dakinis, and Dharma protectors in limitless numbers, all in the aspect of the supporting and supported mandalas of Vajrayogini. They descend close to you and become a single supporting and supported mandala that is similar to the one you have visualized. Imagining this is **concentration**.[46]

In that way, you invoke the wisdom beings through mantra, mudra, and concentration. Once you dissolve them into the commitment being with the extensive mantra of the four doors,[47] you perform the lotus-turning mudra together with the embracing mudra, which the Foremost Great Being [Tsongkhapa] calls "bestowing the essence mudra." The lotus-turning mudra is performed at the heart, and in the Mardo[48] tradition it is initially performed to the left, then the right, and then in the center. Mal Lotsawa[49] calls this "the five aspects of desire" and says that they are performed in the center, to the left, in the center, to the right, and in the center. Either way you chose to do it is acceptable.

[Regarding the mantra], by proclaiming OM YOGA… as well as "All phenomena…" you should be thinking, "Through all worlds and their beings within samsara and nirvana dissolving into me, I am the pure nature of suchness appearing clearly as the supporting and supported mandalas of Vajrayogini." The Sakyapas call the previous [blazing] mudra [performed during PHAIM] the "amazing illusory mudra." The [Sanskrit term for this mudra,] "dzala," has a multitude of meanings, such as "blazing," "to split open," "door," "fish mudra," "illusory," and so forth. From among them, if we translate it as "illusory," and call it "amazing," it becomes a profound practice. However, this mudra is in the aspect of a blazing fire, so Je Rinpoche says that if we translate it as "blazing," that is best.

46. These three terms in bold—mantra, mudra, and concentration—are the three essential features of invoking wisdom beings.

47. This mantra does not appear in Pabongkha Rinpoche's text. The concise edition of this mantra is DZA, HUM, BAM, HO.

48. This refers to the translator Marpa Chökyi Wangchug, also known as Marpa Dopa (ca. 1043–1138).

49. Malgyo Lodro Drag (exact dates uncertain; however, he lived sometime during the eleventh century). For more information on the two translators Mardo and Malgyo, see David Gray, *The Chakrasamvara Tantra: The Discourse of Shri Heruka* (New York: American Institute of Buddhist Studies at Columbia University, 2007).

How to Mix the Three Messengers

They are called "messenger," and "courier," and [this] is similar to a term used for someone who quickly fulfills your desired aims. If they function to quickly lead you along the path, they are called "messenger." Furthermore, once a woman trains her mind in the common path and begins to develop realizations of the generation stage and higher, she becomes an actual mantra-born yogini. While practicing the yoga of purifying migrating beings, you visualize all living beings as yoginis, which is a similitude of mantra-born yoginis. Both of these are lesser outer messengers. Those that dwell in the twenty-four holy places are middling field-born dakinis. Those that dwell in Akanishta are the supreme simultaneously born yoginis. These are the **three outer messengers**. Those that dwell in the thirty-two channels are the lesser inner messengers. Those at the four channels of the heart are the middling. Those in the central channel are the supreme. These are the **three inner messengers**. When your subjective mind becomes the nature of bliss that ascertains emptiness whereby it becomes inseparable bliss and emptiness, which includes the conviction of being the resultant truth body, [this] is the lesser secret messenger. Simultaneously born bliss that realizes a generic image of emptiness as example clear light is the middling. Simultaneously born bliss that directly realizes emptiness as meaning clear light is the supreme. These are the **three secret messengers**.

Therefore, once you invoke the three outer messengers in the aspect of Vajrayogini and you dissolve them into the three inner messengers and so on, [your channels, winds, and drops] are blessed into a state of serviceability whereby, if you sequentially develop the three secret messengers in your mental continuum, it is called "mixing the three messengers," which is evident in the teachings.

Wearing the Armor

Just as there were two systems mentioned earlier for being blessed by the heroes and heroines, so there are also two systems utilized here, with the latter being best. Regarding this, the sadhana states "Upon the moon mandalas at my places…" and continues up to "the nature of Chandika." As for the necessity of wearing the armor, just as a hero enters battle wearing armor such as a coat of mail and helmet to protect him from external weapons, so in this practice we wear armor for the sake of protecting us from harm caused by malignant and interfering spirits. Regarding the basis upon where you place the armor, although Morchen [Kunga Lhundrub, 1654–1728] states that it is arranged on the outer yogini as well as all the principal and retinue deities of the body mandala, Je Rinpoche states that while practicing the [Chakrasamvara systems] of Luipa and Ghantapa, it is permissible for it to be arranged on the outer principal, without the need to arrange it on the body-mandala [deities]. Therefore, in this practice it is also permissible to [merely] arrange it on yourself as the outer yogini.

Regarding the way to arrange it, it is set on the surface of upright moon mandalas that are between skin and muscle, which is clearly explained in the manuscript. Je Rinpoche explains that "arranged at the mouth" means "arranged at the throat," in between the skin and muscle at the Adam's apple. In this practice, the first letters [in the pair], such as OM and so on, are the nature of Vairochana and so forth, and are the seed syllables of the Fathers. The second letters in the pair, such as BAM and so on, are the nature of Varahi and so on, and are the seed syllables of the Mothers. With respect to why the [Mothers' mantras] appear second, despite the fact that the armor mantras are being utilized in relation to the Principal Mother, it is because the Mother is the factor of wisdom on the side of emptiness, so it is primarily utilized on the left.[50] More-over, according to the protecting armor of Vajravidarana, if we observe the light rays in detail, we imagine them only in the aspect of syllables. Regarding this, this is the abode of the profound and secret oral instruc-tions of Mahasiddha Lavapa, so this is exactly how we should do it.

In that way, there are the twenty-four abodes of the inner channels, the eight doors of the sense powers, the four channel petals in the four directions at the heart, and the central channel, through which flow the

---

50. When the Mothers' seed syllables are arranged in the second position on the moon man-dalas, they appear on the left-hand side.

thirty-seven channels and elements, which are visualized as the thirty-seven deities of the body mandala. You invoke all phenomena of cyclic existence and the peace of nirvana as the nature of the three messengers and so forth, which dissolve into you. The ultimate deity is the exalted wisdom of bliss and emptiness appearing in the aspect of mantra-syllables together with their light rays, so wearing the armor that pervades all the spaces between your skin and muscle bestows great power. You are praying, "May I remain undisturbed by any harm whatsoever, such as external obstructing spirits from above, below, and in between; internal obstructions from the aggregation of wind, bile, and phlegm; and so forth."

During the concise self-generation, after generating the deity, you visualize the lord of the lineage as self-arising. At this point during the extensive practice, you should perform the extensive bestowal of empowerment, sealing, offerings, and praises.

ARMOR MANTRA PLACEMENT

Praying for the Yoga of Verbal Recitation and Mental Recitation

This is expressed in the dedication prayer, which states:

> Through verbal and mental recitation focused single-pointedly upon
> The mantra circles at the dharma wheel and emanation wheel,
> And the two incidental completion-stage messengers,
> May I induce simultaneously born bliss and emptiness.

Regarding this, the sadhana states "At my heart..." and continues up through [the italicized instructions that end with the words] *"place your mind in meditative equipoise of bliss and emptiness."*[51] Moreover, regard-

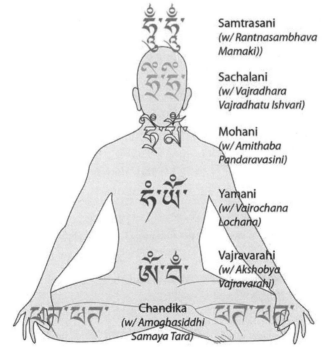

Samtrasani
(w/ Rantnasambhava Mamaki))

Sachalani
(w/ Vajradhara Vajradhatu Ishvari)

Mohani
(w/ Amithaba Pandaravasini)

Yamani
(w/ Vairochana Lochana)

Vajravarahi
(w/ Akshobya Vajravarahi)

Chandika
(w/ Amoghasiddhi Samaya Tara)

ARMOR MANTRA-SYLLABLES WITH EXPLANATIONS

51. Pabongkha Dechen Nyingpo, *The Extremely Secret Dakini of Naropa*, p. 298.

ing **verbal recitation**, you should recite in a whisper so that others cannot hear you. Therefore, when meditating on the body mandala, if you don't meditate on the Principal Mother of that [body mandala], you visualize the phenomena source, moon, syllable BAM, and mantra rosary directly in the center of your chest, between the two breasts of the outer Vajrayogini. This is the heap recitation. In the text it is clear that the commitment recitation is the primary recitation, for which you focus single-pointedly without letting your mind waver from the visualization to something else and without the eight faults.[52] In this way, you recite as many [mantras] as you can, or at least the number that you have promised [to recite each day], which is why it is called the "commitment recitation." This is the means of protecting the commitments you promised to keep during the empowerment and functions to accomplish the aims of yourself and others, which is the general commitment of a buddha; therefore it is called "commitment recitation." Once you collect the power of all the buddhas' blessings as the means of accomplishing your own welfare, your own mental continuum is blessed. And by touching others with light rays and so on, as a means of accomplishing the welfare of others whereby you purify the negative karma and obscurations of all living beings, you imagine that their bodies are transformed into uncontaminated enjoyment bodies of Vajrayogini and their minds transform into the nonconceptual truth body. The term "uncontaminated" also means the pure illusory body arisen from meaning clear light; and "nonconceptual" means that we currently have a multitude of conceptions that only give rise to

---

52. Pabongkha Rinpoche's commentary to Chittamani Tara, *Secret Revelations of Chittamani Tara* (Dechen Ling Press, 2013), pp. 74–75, explains the eight faults: "*The Tantra Requested by Subhahu* states:

> When proclaiming the mantra, don't recite too quickly, too slowly,
> Not too loudly and not too softly;
> Don't converse with others and don't be distracted,
> Or [recite] the anusvara and visarga improperly.

Thus don't recite the mantra extremely quickly so that it is as though the sounds of the syllables are piled one upon another. You also shouldn't recite each and every syllable extremely slowly. Don't recite it so loudly that others can hear you or so softly that you yourself can't hear it. Don't interrupt your recitation with ordinary speech. Don't let your mind become distracted. Recite the vowels properly as well as the anusvara and visarga. Thus you should recite the mantra free from these eight faults."

more conceptualizations, and although all conceptions cease during the clear light of death, we are unable to sustain this for very long and instead accomplish the intermediate state. Not only that, but although the tenth-ground bodhisattvas and so forth are able to cease conceptualizations during meditative stabilization, they cannot do so during subsequent attainment. At the time of the path as well, although conceptions cease when the isolated mind of example clear light manifests, when you cannot remain in that clear light, the impure illusory body is accomplished from the contaminated wind. That very illusory body disappears like a cloud in the sky when you manifest meaning clear light. And although the delusion-obstructions are abandoned at that time [of meaning clear light], you have not attained the actual union, so with the uncontaminated wind of five-colored lights functioning as the substantial cause, you arise as the pure illusory body. This is not the pure illusory body that you trained with during the previous paths, nor is this the clear light of the past. Instead, when you attain the actual union that has unified the pair of body and mind as one, it is as it says: "Whatever activities you undertake, it is complete pacification of conceptual thoughts." When you remain unwavering from meditative equipoise on the truth body-mind by blending meditation and subsequent attainment, you effortlessly work for the welfare of all living beings; therefore "uncontaminated" is the resultant truth body.

Regarding **mental recitation**, you recite without moving your tongue or lips. Moreover, according to the former systems, you engage in a scanning meditation on the completion stage subsequent to mental recitation. However, according to the intention of Changkya [Rolpai Dorje], you perform mental recitation subsequent to the first scanning meditation on the completion stage. To practice the **first scanning meditation on the completion stage**, begin by sitting with the sevenfold essential bodily postures [of Vairochana], and dispel the stale winds through the nine-round breathing. If you have [been visualizing] the body mandala, sequentially dissolve it from the edges and meditate on the body as an empty shell. Directly in the center of your body is the central channel with four characteristics,[53] with the phenomena

---

53. The four characteristics are: 1) red and oily, like liquid resin, 2) clear and luminous, like

source and so forth within the very center of your heart. Imagine that this descends to your navel, and once you conjoin the winds, focus on the four joy-swirls at the four corners of the phenomena source that are spinning while your mind remains focused on the syllable BAM, which is on the verge of bursting into flames.

To practice **mental recitation**, once again bring the winds into embrace at the navel, after which your mind as the syllable BAM reads the mantra rosary counterclockwise. This meditation alone is most definitely a means of igniting the great bliss of the generation stage. However, according to the intention of Changkya Rinpoche, it is excellent if you do this meditation because through visualizing the three channels, the four channel wheels, and so on you also induce the great bliss of the completion stage. This is my Venerable Guru [Ngulchu Dharmabhadra]'s way of practicing, and he would occasionally do it in conjunction with the three rounds of mixing and so forth.

Therefore, to practice the **second scanning meditation on the completion stage**, bring the phenomena source at your navel upward through your central channel to your heart, and dissolve it sequentially from its edges inward into emptiness. Visualize the red and white joy-swirls at the upper and lower ends of your central channel. While your mind is absorbed in the red joy-swirl at the lower end [of your central channel], it moves upward through the inner passageway of your central channel, whereby your body and mind become blissful. With your mind at the upper end [of your central channel], the white joy-swirl descends through the inner passageway of your central channel and all appearances dissipate. These two mix at your heart and become a counterclockwise whirling pink joy-swirl that becomes increasingly smaller until it disappears into emptiness and you place your mind in a state of bliss and emptiness. Next, you should perform the inconceivable contemplations through the path of the body mandala and so forth. If those persons with extremely sharp faculties wish to practice [the two scanning meditations and the mental recitation] in conjunction with the body mandala, it is very clearly presented in the manuscripts.

---

a lamp of sesame oil, 3) straight and true, like the trunk of a plantain tree, and 4) soft and flexible, like the petals of a lotus.

In that way, focus your attention single-pointedly upon the mantra wheel within the dharma wheel at your heart, which is the abode of your extremely subtle wind-and-mind that is the source of all phenomena, and perform verbal recitation. The luminous red element at your navel that you obtained from your mother functions as the cause for your body to "generate" and "emanate," and itself is the basis of generating and emanating bliss [and is therefore called "the emanation wheel"]. Focus your visualization single-pointedly upon the mantra wheel at the emanation wheel at your navel, engage in mental recitation, and unify the generation stage and the scanning completion stage. Thus you are praying, "Through this, may I easily be able to induce the exalted wisdom of simultaneously born bliss and emptiness through such a messenger."

Praying for the Common Yoga of Inconceivability

This is expressed in the dedication prayer, which states:

> May my mind abide in the sphere of bliss and emptiness when,
> Through the lasso light rays emanating from the syllable BAM
>   and mantra rosary,
> The worlds and their beings of the three realms melt into light
>   and dissolve into me
> And I also sequentially dissolve into emptiness.

The sadhana states "Light rays radiate from the BAM..." and continues up to "transforms into unobservable emptiness." Furthermore, red light rays radiate from the syllable BAM and mantra rosary at the heart of either yourself or the Principal Mother of the body mandala, and by merely touching the formless realm, the form realm, and the desire realm, they melt into blue, red, and white light rays, just like putting salt granules in water, and sequentially contract inward from the edges. The [formless, form, and desire realms] dissolve into your body [in three stages]: from your neck upward, from your neck down to your navel, and below your navel, [respectively]. When the desire realm dissolves, you also dissolve the mountain of fire, up to Bhairava and Kalarati, into your lower sections. You also dissolve into the phenomena source upon the nada of the BAM. That also dissolves into pristine emptiness like a rainbow disappearing, whereby your mind becomes the nature of great bliss through which the subjective emptiness ascertains the [objective] emptiness of inherent existence, whereby subject and object become one taste and that [state of] bliss and emptiness is placed in meditative equipoise on the truth body. In that way you are praying, "May my mind itself be able to remain in the sphere of bliss and emptiness once the hooking red rays of light that emanate from my mind, together with the syllable BAM and mantra rosary that are the nature of great bliss, dissolve all worlds and their beings into the aspect of blue, red, and white light rays and they dissolve into the upper, middle, and lower parts of my body, in dependence upon which I also sequentially dissolve into the emptiness of the mind itself."

The Yoga of Daily Actions

At this point, you practice the actual yoga of daily actions together with its limbs. Regarding the first of these two, the sadhana states "From within that state of emptiness..." and continues up to "protected by the terrifying mudra." In the Sakya tradition they call this "the yoga of mental stabilization" and "the yoga without mental stabilization." The Gelugpas call this "the yoga of actual session" and "the yoga of the session break"; however, they have the same meaning, so it is called "the yoga of daily actions" [here], which is synonymous with the second term just mentioned. Furthermore, according to the former explanation, you arise from that previous state of meditative equipoise of bliss and emptiness in the aspect of Vajrayogini with ornaments but without hand implements, and protect yourself by wearing the armor. Protecting the environment is accomplished with the SUMBHANI mantra and by performing the terrifying mudra. This is the mantra of the deity Sumbha and contains four HUMs; therefore it is called "the mantra of the four HUMs" and "the mantra of the four faces" because it is proclaimed by the four faces of Heruka.

Next, set your intention to engage in virtuous practices until you begin your next session. In the interim, rely on mindfulness and continuously check to ensure that your previous intention does not deteriorate before the beginning of your next session. In particular, you should view whatever wrathful manifestations appear as being the three families,[54] put an end to attachment and anger, and regard them as manifestations of the three joys.

For the yoga of **the limbs of yoga**, practice the yoga of eating, the yoga of outer offerings or the tsok offering (ganachakra), the yoga of burnt offerings, the yoga of the tenth-day [offerings], and the yoga of the tormas. I am not going to write more on this for fear of it becoming too verbose; therefore you can learn them from the *Lecture Notes*[55] and so forth.

In that way, once you instantaneously arise from within the state of bliss and emptiness as the deity Vajrayogini displaying the armor with ornaments but without hand implements, you should verbally proclaim the terrifying sound of the mantra, like the simultaneous roar of a thousand thunderclaps that manifests from the aspect of the fire of exalted wisdom of bliss and emptiness, which radiates to the ten directions and protects you from all outer, inner, and secret obstacles. Additionally, you are praying, "May I not make a partial attempt but thoroughly complete the yoga of daily actions as well as its yoga of the branches, by viewing whatever appears to my six senses as manifestations of the guru-deity's three secrets of body, speech, and mind."

Praying to Accomplish the Result of the Generation Stage has two sections:

1) THE ACTUAL PRAYER TO ACCOMPLISH THE RESULT OF THE GENERATION STAGE
2) PRAYING FOR THE SPECIAL MEANS OF ACCOMPLISHING THE RESULT OF THE GENERATION STAGE

54. There are various ways of presenting the lineages, or "families," of enlightened beings. The most common is as the five buddha families, with each family related to each one of the five aggregates of an individual as form, feeling, discrimination, compositional factors, and consciousness. Another method is to reduce them to three families, where Akshobya represents the mind, Amitabha represents the speech, and Vairochana represents the body.

55. "*Lecture Notes*" refers to Ngulchu Dharmabhadra's text on the generation and completion stages of Vajrayogini, which consists of notes from those attending his lecture, compiled by his disciple Losang Tsering and entitled "rJe bstun rdo rje rnal 'byor ma'i bskyed rdzogs kyi zin bris mkha' spyod bgrod pa'i gsang lam snying gi thig le."

The Actual Prayer to Accomplish the Result of the Generation Stage has two sections:

1) Praying to Accomplish Dakini Land without Abandoning Your Body
2) Praying to Be Cared for in the Intermediate State and All Future Lives

Praying to Accomplish Dakini Land without Abandoning Your Body has two sections:

1) Those of Supreme Faculties Praying to Be Liberated through Mere Meditation and Recitation
2) Those of Middling Faculties Praying to Be Liberated in Dependence upon the Langaliya Stem

Those of Supreme Faculties Praying to Be Liberated through Mere Meditation and Recitation

This is expressed in the dedication prayer, which states:

> Thus, through the yoga of the directions and the moon,
> One day, may I be led directly to the City of Knowledge-Holders
> By the coral-colored goddess of joy with free-flowing
> Vermillion hair and moving orange eyes.

The teachings state, "The supreme method for accomplishing outer Dakini Land is this generation stage of Vajravarahi together with verbal recitation, for which you definitely do not need to rely upon the completion stage; therefore it is called 'the generation stage of Varahi of Dakini Land.'" However, what this means is that you practice [at the same time] a union of the generation and completion stages; therefore this practice is vastly superior to other generation-stage practices.[56]

Moreover, you should incorporate the four empowerments into the body of the path, which has an aspect concordant with experiencing

56. In deity practices other than Heruka and Vajrayogini, it is stated that you must first perfect the generation stage and only then can you practice the completion stage. However, in Vajrayogini and Heruka you practice the generation and the completion stages simultaneously.

and accumulating karma once you have taken rebirth. After you have generated and dissolved the guru, from merely a mental perspective, you generate yourself as Vajrayogini complete with the four attributes through the skillful means of bringing death, the intermediate state, and rebirth into the path as the three bodies of the Conqueror as the actual basis of purification—which constitutes the actual generation stage— through manifesting the phenomena source, moon, mantra rosary, seed syllable, and so forth from within the state of emptiness. In that way, the mantra circle at the heart symbolizes that you should encircle the complete path of the generation stage with the mantra wheel of the generation stage. The outer phenomena source of the heart[57] symbolizes the protection wheel; the inner [phenomena source] symbolizes the charnel grounds; the moon symbolizes the hero; and the mantra rosary, [including the first five syllables, namely,] short-AH, YA, RA, LA, and WA, symbolize the heroine. Everything thus far symbolizes the path of the vase empowerment.

During the completion stage, the three channels, the five channel wheels, and the red and white elements in their center symbolize the charnel grounds. The winds entering, abiding, and dissolving and so on are the means of making your channels, winds, and drops serviceable, whereby you actualize the exalted wisdoms of appearance, increase, and near-attainment through which you complete the actual illusory body accomplished from mere wind and mind. Regarding this, the actual completion stage of the conventional illusory body and all its paths of the completion stage are symbolized by the mantra wheel at your heart.

The outer phenomena source at your heart symbolizes thirty-two channel petals of the bliss-sustaining wheel at your secret place. The inner [phenomena source] symbolizes the sixty-four channel petals of the emanation wheel at your navel. The moon symbolizes the eight channel petals of the dharma wheel at your heart. The syllable BAM and the four joy-swirls symbolize the sixteen channel petals of the enjoyment wheel at your throat. The mantra rosary symbolizes the thirty-two channel petals

---

57. When visualizing the body mandala, there are two phenomena sources at your heart. The inner phenomena source is within the heart of the Principal Mother of the body mandala, and the outer phenomena source is the abode of the body-mandala deities and is within the heart of yourself as the outer Principal Mother.

of the wheel of great bliss at your crown. Meditating on them all at your heart symbolizes the effectiveness of penetrating the essential points of the four channel wheels. The two phenomena sources symbolize the channel wheels of your body. The BAM and mantra rosary symbolize the syllables of the channel wheels. The moon symbolizes the mandala of the nectar-elements. Holding the winds in embrace symbolizes the effectiveness of penetrating the essential points of the channel wheel of wind at the heart. All together, these symbolize the secret empowerment.

The outer and inner methods symbolize that the exalted wisdom of great bliss emerges from increasing the excellent method of accomplishing the serviceability of your channels, winds, and drops. That exalted wisdom symbolizes generating the simultaneously born exalted wisdom as the actual definitive meaning of Vajrayogini caused by directly realizing emptiness, which is ultimate clear light and the actual completion stage, and which symbolizes that the two incidental completion stages contain all paths of that completion stage. In dependence upon the "upper Dakini Land" of the four white joy-swirls, you attain nonconceptual emptiness. In dependence upon the mandala of the lower wind of the red joy-swirl, you accomplish bliss. In dependence upon the outer mantra wheel at your heart, which lies in between [the upper and lower joy-swirls]—and in particular upon the syllable BAM and its nada, which is on the verge of bursting into flames—you accomplish heat. Uniting the upper and lower joy-swirls at your heart, they dissipate into emptiness, whereby you generate the exalted wisdom of inseparable bliss and emptiness that is the path of the wisdom empowerment. Visualizing your body as Vajrayogini at that time accomplishes the pure illusory body, and imagining your mind as inseparable bliss and emptiness accomplishes the pure mind of meaning clear light. The union of unifying body and mind as one is the path of the fourth empowerment. This is the concentration of "migrating to glory" or, to use another term, "inconceivability."

In that way, you utilize skillfulness by stringing together as one the canonical description of the practice, so that it contains the complete path of the four empowerments and functions as a purifying agent of the basis of purification.

Once you establish a foundation of training your mind in the common path and perfectly safeguarding your vows and commitments, you then practice without break. Build the foundation further by completing a retreat of four-hundred-thousand [mantras] and the burnt offering, and if you assiduously perform the two tenth-day offerings and the tsok offering, before too long, without having to forsake this body, you will be led to Dakini Land by women who are emanations of Venerable Vajrayogini. Therefore, the term "Thus" is like a name used as an initiating verbal designation whose meaning immediately transcends its conventional expression. The term "directions" is in exact accordance with the former explanation and is the name for "ten," while "moon" is the name for "one," and if you properly practice the yogas of "ten" and "one," one day before too long, you will meet an excellent woman who is an emanation of Vajrayogini and who is distinguished by an extremely red complexion like a coral. Her orange hair is similar to the color of sindhura and is unbound and flowing freely. She has orange eyebrows, and her eyes dart about. The skin on her forehead has a pattern in the shape of a joy-swirl. Once you meet her, you should realize with complete certainty that she is an emanation of the Venerable Mother. Merely relying upon supplicating her with substances, mantras, and so forth will be enough for you to go to Dakini Land. Your experiences of Dakini Land will not be like a dream but will be directly perceived. In that very body you will be certain to attain the supreme attainment. Thus you are praying, "May I be cared for and led by the hand to Dakini Land as the City of Knowledge-Holders."

Those of Middling Faculties Praying to Be Liberated in Dependence upon the Langaliya Stem

This is expressed in the dedication prayer, which states:

> Practicing in a land of corpses with a langali[ya] stem filled
> With sindhura, and wandering throughout all the lands,
> May the beautiful goddess to whom the joy-swirl
> Between my eyebrows transfers lead me to Dakini Land.

Moreover, in accordance with the previous explanation, those of supreme faculties [can accomplish Dakini Land] by mere recitation and mediation, yet when, despite your great optimism, you are not liberated through [these] alone, you should perform the practice of sindhura. Therefore, you should practice retreat, accomplishment, and the application of activities according to the *Lecture Notes*. During its accomplishment until the present moment of the sindhura mandala, you have been establishing the cause so that you will able to succeed in this practice [of finding an emanation of Vajrayogini]. During recitation you recite "Within the red double-tetrahedron phenomena source at the heart of the front-generation," after which you engage in the general visualization of [mantra] recitation. In particular, with the simultaneously born messenger acting as the principal [deity], you summon the mental continua of the messengers of the ten directions. Once you summon limitless numbers of them in the aspect of Vajrayogini, you should repeatedly contemplate that they dissolve into the heart of the front-generation as well as the seed syllable and mantra rosary, whereby you subjugate all the messengers by appropriately delighting them.

Although the term "dogopa"[58] is understood to mean Indian rhubarb,[59] it means a large stalk of mendowa,[60] so if you can't obtain it there is nothing wrong with using Indian rhubarb. You need an assistant to keep watch, and he should have a club that is a half an arm span in length. You can ascertain its appropriate length by placing the fingertips of your two hands at the level of your heart so that they touch and measuring the distance from there to the end of your elbow. This has the same meaning as a cubit. Regarding its shape, its substance is kept secret but it is definitely round, and although its size it not explained, any size is acceptable.

In that way, once you perform the completely perfect retreat as a preliminary, by reciting the three-OM mantra of Venerable Vajrayogini three million two-hundred-thousand times, nine million six-hundred-thousand [times], or simply ten million [times],[61] you engage in the practice of the langaliya stem without making mistakes as to the substances

---

58. Tib. *do rgod pa*. I have been unable to ascertain exactly what type of plant this is. Pabongkha Rinpoche says "it is shaped like a flattened pandit's hat and has yellow flowers."

59. Tib. *lcum*. Latin *rheum palmatum*. It is a type of Indian rhubarb.

60. Tib. s*man do ba*.

61. Pabongkha Rinpoche's retreat instructions state that although other retreat manuals state that you can recite 9,600,000 mantras, in the Gaden tradition you must recite 10,000,000 mantras for an extensive great retreat.

and ways of practice. In Sanskrit this [substance] is called "sindhura," and in Tibetan "leetri." Thus you are praying, "By practicing in a charnel ground with corpses, wandering around in all directions, and continuing my search regardless of whether I become rich or poor, am in ascent or decline, have success or failure, may I be led to the abode of Pure Dakini Land by the beautiful maiden to whom the joy-swirl design on my forehead has transferred so that now she has the sindhura drawing on her forehead."

Praying to Be Cared for in the Intermediate State and All Future Lives

This is expressed in the dedication prayer, which states:

> Even if I am not liberated in this life, through the force of
> Applying myself single-pointedly in meditation, recitation, and
>   so forth,
> May the Joyous Goddess of Dakini Land take me under her care
> During the intermediate state or before too long.

In accordance with the previous explanation, if despite practicing recitation, meditation, accomplishing the sindhura, and so forth you don't accomplish realizations, or if despite practicing in that way you are not capable of traveling to Dakini Land in this life without abandoning your body, you are a person of lesser faculties. And even if that doesn't come to pass, if you don't fall prey to laziness but proceed without any hesitation and entrust yourself completely[62] and uninterruptedly to the practice of the Venerable Mother, [then] as it says in the *Heruka Root Tantra*, you will be escorted through the intermediate state by the heroes and yoginis to Dakini Land. Nevertheless, if you don't reach attainments because you are unable to practice in that way, due to laziness and other circumstances, [then] you are a person of the least of the lesser faculties. Yet even in that case, once you receive a perfectly qualified empowerment

---

62. In Tibetan the phrase reads "lungs, heart, and chest" (*glo snying brang gsum*), which means to entrust yourself fully to something.

and blessing permission, if your vows and commitments have not deteriorated—or if, despite having deteriorated, you are able to prepare by confessing your transgression at the time of death and either receive an empowerment or take self-initiation, depending on which is more suitable—[then] you will restore your vows and commitments. And, if you are not defiled by a root downfall, it is said that you will accomplish the supreme attainment within three, five, or, at the very least, sixteen lives. Therefore, the term "if" indicates these two reasons [mentioned above].

Thus you are praying, "If, despite my efforts in meditation, recitation, and so forth, I am unable to attain certain liberation in that body through being led to Dakini Land in that life, even then I will not succumb to laziness or entertain doubts but, in dependence upon the power of my single-pointed efforts, may I come under the care of Venerable Vajrayogini, the Joyous Goddess of Dakini Land, and either be escorted to Dakini Land from the abode of the intermediate state by heroes and dakinis or, even if I don't attain that, without having to wait too long, may I accomplish it in sixteen lives at the very least."

Praying for the Special Means of Accomplishing the Result of the Generation Stage has two sections:

1) Praying for the Yoga of the Quick Path of Transference of Consciousness
2) Praying for the Uncommon Yoga of Inconceivability

Praying for the Yoga of the Quick Path of Transference of Consciousness

This is revealed in the dedication prayer, which states:

> When the "mount of odor" wind quickly moves my mind, in the
> form of a syllable BAM,
> Up my central channel and through the door of Brahma,
> May I attain instant liberation through the death-time path
> Of mixing with the Mother of the Conqueror's mind of bliss
> and emptiness.

Moreover, this is the very instruction on transference of consciousness (phowa). There are four [types of] practitioners [mentioned earlier]: 1) supreme, 2) middling, 3) lesser, and 4) those of the very least capacity. This practice is intended for the last type. Furthermore, with the exception of being reborn in the formless realm, everyone experiences the intermediate state. In the intermediate state of persons of least capacity, despite the fact that they are escorted by heroes and dakinis, they must still accomplish an intermediate state. Therefore, it is said they don't have to experience the fear and trepidation of [the intermediate state]. However, Tsarchen said that this is from the perspective of those of the very least capacity. Je Rinpoche comments on this by calling it "the shortcut path." If you are unable to make it to Dakini Land in this life, once you take rebirth in a physical form for the practice of Mantra, you will need to practice the remainder of the path to Dakini Land and so forth in a future life. If you don't attain such a physical basis due to the onslaught of obstacles, you can still attain a physical basis for the practice of Mantra through transference of consciousness and are therefore capable of cutting short the obstacles to the path.

For this, the previous beings also asserted two types of practice of transference of consciousness: that of the Father, which relies upon the Father and Mother in embrace, as well as transference of consciousness, which relies upon the Solitary Mother. Later they introduced three practices: one with the Father as the Solitary Father, one with the Mother as the Solitary Mother, and one in dependence upon the Father and Mother in embrace. For the reliance upon the Solitary Mother there are also two, the common and uncommon. With respect to the second one, the transference of consciousness of [the Dakini] Niguma calls it "enlightenment without meditation," with a dual internal division of the white and red flowers. Naropa's Goddess of Dakini Land itself has three transference of consciousness practices for which you practice the heart-essence of all the profound oral instructions that have been combined as one. Once these are explained to a few people in strict retreat, you undertake whichever practice you prefer for a month, twenty-one days, and so on until special signs occur that you have accomplished Dakini Land, such as the retreat house and your body being struck by a rainbow, a rain of sindhura and flowers descending, a sweet scent emerging without any cause, or a swelling on the crown of your head with pus and blood dripping from it. Therefore, you should not forget the training you undertook; however, if you practice "applying the action" before you are on the brink of passing away, it is said that "transference of consciousness will shorten your life" and will damage your lifespan. In that way, the means of training in transference of consciousness, applying the action, and so forth are taught in the *Lecture Notes*.[63] Through practicing in this way, the phrase "the quickly moving mount of odor" is used, and the teachings state that "the moving 'mount of odor' wind is like a forest." Accordingly, the wind moves through the quickly changing mount of odor, your mind is visualized in the form of the syllable BAM, and once it moves through the passageway of the path of the central channel, [or] avadhuti, it arrives at the door of the Brahma aperture at the crown of your head, leaves, and mixes with the mind of the Mother of the Conquerors, Vajrayogini, which is inseparable bliss and emptiness. Thus you are praying, "May I be able to quickly attain liberation through practicing the quick path of the yoga of transference of consciousness at the moment of my death, at the very instant my body and mind separate."

Praying for the Uncommon Yoga of Inconceivability

This is revealed in the dedication prayer, which states:

> When the inner Varahi has destroyed the creeping vine of apprehender and apprehended,
> And the dancing goddess dwelling within my supreme central channel
> Exits the crown of my head into the sphere of space,
> May she frolic in embrace with the Hero Blood-Drinker.

The teachings refer to this as "the three oral instructions at the time of the dawning of nonduality," and [this] is the third oral instruction. The term "oral instruction" indicates that it must be learned orally by

---

63. For an extensive explanation of everything mentioned above, see Pabongkha Dechen Nyingpo, *The Extremely Secret Dakini of Naropa* (Snow Lion, 2011).

striving to please a holy guru, and means that it is a secret precept of the Hearing Lineage. In general, it is practiced in secret and discretely; therefore it is called "Secret Mantra." Every practice related to Mantra, and in particular this general cycle of teachings of this Venerable Mother and this special oral instruction itself, possesses four essential features of the Hearing Lineage. If the unbroken lineage [of the Hearing Lineage] is not attained, then even though a person may have obtained the empowerments of Heruka, Hevajra, and so on, as well as the blessing of the Venerable Mother, it is inappropriate to carelessly teach it to such a person. Moreover, the three terms "inner Dakini Land," "great Dakini Land," and "the state of union" are synonymous. If you aspire to such states, you must also perfect the coarse and subtle generation stage, and in accordance with the first inconceivability, [this must be] followed by the training in the completion stage. However, you must [also] first perfect the coarse and subtle generation stages if you aspire to *outer* Dakini Land through other highest yoga tantra practices, after which you are capable of attaining the common attainments, such as the eight great attainments as the preparation for Dakini Land and so forth. Yet in this practice, those with supreme faculties don't need to perfect the coarse [generation stage]. Instead, through performing a retreat, together with the compensating burnt offering and properly protecting their vows and commitments—and if they practice initial preparation of this inconceivability—they can accomplish Dakini Land through this skillful means. In general, you can accomplish Dakini Land by: 1) relying upon the Father, 2) relying upon the Mother, or 3) relying upon the birth of a "seventh born." The term "seventh born" means someone born seven times as a pure brahman or seven times as a pure bhikshu.[64] However, the *Heruka Root Tantra* explains that this refers to someone who has taken seven uninterrupted rebirths as a human from one life to the other, and it is the flesh of this person that is being referred to as "the flesh of a seventh born." In actuality, the *Root Tantra* states that you should take the consecration of[65] his heart that is similar to the color of saffron, which some lamas say is like the yellow-colored water that fills a balloon.

64. Tib. *dge slong*. A bhikshu is a fully ordained Buddhist monk maintaining 253 vows.
65. Tib. *ro tsa na*.

As a sign of such a person, the disposition of those people is peaceful and they have little anger, they blink only very seldom, their bodies and mouths have a sweet scent, and their shadows will have seven layers. With respect to the way of moving, their activities are similar to the [graceful] way a goose moves; these are the signs of those who have consecration [in their hearts]. Regarding the way to respond to that, some of those people have great moral strength of bodhichitta; therefore they are said to be like a treasure and you should not use their bodies.[66]

Also, because it is stated that by applying the action [of taking consecration] you engage in killing, the Foremost Great Being [Tsongkhapa] states that this is forbidden, but that if they die naturally, you can extract the consecration from their hearts. Engage in a preliminary retreat, and by utilizing that mantra, apply the [blood from the consecrated heart] to your forehead. If you do, you will accomplish the attainment of Dakini Land.

[Accomplishing Dakini Land] relying upon the Mother has both common and uncommon methods. Regarding the first [common method], recite as many mantras as you are able in conjunction with the generation stage of this practice. Regarding the uncommon, this practice is clearly revealed in the *Lecture Notes* concerning the [uncommon yoga of] inconceivability. This is also called "the inner Varahi" and was composed in

66. This is a reference to the eleventh chapter of the *Chakrasamvara Root Tantra*, which states:
"Furthermore, these things will occur:
By the practitioner merely relying [on this]
Person born seven times [as a human]
It is taught that you will quickly induce the attainments
And accomplish all realizations.
The person from whom a sweet scent of perspiration arises, [who] speaks the truth and has not closed his eyes for a long time, does not become angry, and whose breath is very delicious, that person has taken a human rebirth seven times. His manner of walking is without the seven defilements and he is endowed with flawless compassion.
   In dependence upon such a person, extracting his heart and reciting the essence mantra of Glorious Heruka one hundred and eight times and forming a drop, you will fly, travelling ten million miles. By merely relying on that you will quickly come to possess the exalted wisdom of the three worlds. You will travel back and forth five million miles in one day and one night. You will attain the body of the deity, what is known to be the essence of Heruka. Whatever one desires will be bestowed." Chapter 11 of the *Chakrasamvara Root Tantra*, p. 54, as translated by David Gonsalez (Dechen Ling Press, 2010; available through the DLP website).

conjunction with transference of consciousness by Rigzin Pema Trinlay[67] and consists of one folio. While my Venerable Guru [Ngulchu Dharma-bhadra] was giving a discourse, he mentioned that he thought that perhaps the prayer for the uncommon yoga of inconceivability is Tsarchen's own intention, and used this as his means of giving an extensive commentary.

With respect to the "inner Varahi," she is the red element within the center of the channel wheel at your navel that is the nature of Vajra-yogini. Duplicates emanate from that on the tips of light rays, whereby all apprehended environments and beings, as well as the apprehending conceptual thoughts, are absorbed and dissolve into the Vajrayogini at your navel. Therefore, [*The Hevajra Tantra in Two Chapters Entitled*] *"The Two Examinations"*[68] states:

> The left channel is the nature of wisdom,
> The right channel is the perfect abode of method;
> Thoroughly abandon apprehended and apprehender by
> Abiding in the center of the central channel.

According to this, the body of the outer yogini is sequentially withdrawn from below, while simultaneously the moving wind of the apprehended within your right roma channel is dissolved from the sole of the right foot of the inner yogini.[69] The moving wind of the apprehender within your left kyangma channel dissolves into her left foot. Through these dissolutions, the "creeping vine" of the two moving winds of apprehended and apprehender is overcome. From among the three types of inner messengers, the supreme is accomplished by conjoining [these two winds] into the path of the central channel through which you simultaneously dissolve from the crown of your head to the soles of your feet. She comes to possess a dancing posture in the aspect of levitating like a dancer. Thus you are praying, "When she comes to the Brahma door at the crown of my head and emerges into the pathway of the clouds in the sphere of space,

---

67. I believe this is the famous Nyingma lama Rigzin Pema Trinlay (1641–1717).
68. Tib. *brTag pa gnyis pa*.
69. It is important to remember that the inner yogini is your own mind. Therefore when the term "she" is used in the following paragraph, it is really your own mind.

may she embrace with Heruka 'the Drinker of Blood' and eternally frolic in the exalted wisdom of nondual bliss and emptiness."

Praying to Generate the Realizations of the Completion Stage has two sections:

1) Praying to Generate the Realizations of the Completion Stage in Your Mental Continuum
2) Praying to Accomplish the Results of the Completion Stage

Praying to Generate the Realizations of the Completion Stage in Your Mental Continuum has two sections:

1) Praying to Generate the Great Path of the Central Channel Common to the Solitary Father
2) Praying to Generate the Lesser Path of the Central Channel Uncommon to the Solitary Mother

Praying to Generate the Great Path of the Central Channel Common to the Solitary Father has two sections:

1) Praying for the Yoga of Blessing the Self
2) Praying for the Oral Instructions on the Yoga Inner Fire to Open the Mouth of the Central Channel

Praying for the Yoga of Blessing the Self

This is revealed in the dedication prayer, which states:

> Through the yoga of embrace while meditating single-pointedly
> Upon the seed of the five winds at the lotus of my navel,
> May my mental continuum be satiated by supreme bliss
> Through the wind entering the channels of my body-mind.

Moreover, the teachings state, "The great and lesser completion stages of the central channel primarily accomplish inner Dakini Land." The *Embracing Tantra*[70] states:

> Enlightenment that would otherwise take
> Countless eons to attain
> Can be attained in this life
> If you have supreme bliss.

The path takes a long time in the practice of the sutra system and the three lower classes of tantra, so unless you rely upon the path of highest yoga Mantra, you will not be able to attain the state of union. Although for the best trainees there isn't any difference in superiority or inferiority in all the entirety of sutra and tantra with respect to emptiness as the object of their realization, it is the force of exalted wisdom of simultaneously born great bliss in the mind of the person realizing emptiness that makes it possible to attain the state of Vajradhara in one such life. This is a special defining feature unique to highest yoga tantra. Generating that exalted wisdom is also addressed in the *Heruka Root Tantra* when it states:

> Accomplish the simultaneously born messenger,
> The supreme, middling, and inferior.

The inner messenger, or, in other words, "the supreme goddess of the lineage," is within the center of the channel wheel within the central channel. Other than penetrating the vital points [of the central channel], and unifying wind and mind within it, there is no other means capable of generating that exalted wisdom. Therefore, this practice also reveals the primary means of generating the exalted wisdom of great bliss once you penetrate the vital points of the central channel as a unique feature of highest yoga tantra, and for this reason it is called "the greater and lesser central channel." In that way, this is also the method of assessing the mutual inclusion of the three examples[71] in the practice of the

70. Tib. *Kha sbyor.*
71. Pabongkha Rinpoche explains these three examples in *The Extremely Secret Dakini of Naropa* (Snow Lion, 2011), pp. 226–27: "Furthermore Sakya Drakpa Gyaltsen used

central-channel path of the completion stage, the meaning of which also contains the basis, path, and result. On the path there are also two [modes of teaching]: 1) showing reality directly, and 2) showing reality indirectly. Showing reality indirectly also contains the path free from attachment and the path with attachment. The path with attachment has two classifications: 1) that common to the Father and Mother, and 2) the uncommon. Although the first contains three sections—[namely,] 1) training in winds as a preliminary, 2) the "stage of abiding in the superior self" or, using another term, "the stage of blessing the self," and 3) the yoga of opening the mouth of the central channel—only the first two are outlined in this prayer. The first is referred to as "the lotus of the navel" and is condensed into the first line of the verse. Furthermore, visualize your body as Vajrayogini, in the nature of red light and hollow, in the center of which are the central, right, and left channels in a single sheath, from your navel to your throat. Its circumference is the size of a bamboo or an arrow. From your throat, each of the three channels continues upward, with the central channel terminating at the Brahma aperture and the right and left channels terminating at the openings of the two nostrils. The lower end where they meet up is like a bamboo reed with a blocked end, similar to a flat, swirling, pale-white moon mandala. In its center is a blue drop as the space-wind, in the east is the green drop of wind-wind, in the south is the yellow drop of the earth-wind, in the west is the red drop of fire-wind, and in the north is the white drop of water-wind. They all possess three special qualities of being radiant, solid, and globular. Their size is that of a small pea, or that of a mustard seed, and corresponding to the size of the central one.

Next, when you exhale through the nostrils, imagine that the wind immediately emanates from the central [blue] drop as though it were a long thread of blue smoke that stretches out and emerges from the nostrils. It travels either twelve or sixteen finger-widths in front of you

---

the following three examples in his *Manual of the Central Channel concerning Vajravarahi* [*Phag mo'i skor gyi rtsa dbu ma*]: a lumberjack must be skilled in the essential points of a tree, a butcher in the essential points of life, and a magician in the essential points of illusions. Through these three examples we can understand that we must be skilled in the essential points of the path pertaining to Vajrayogini and penetrating the essential points of the vajra-body."

and becomes a swirl of blue. When the wind reenters, the blue string enters your nostrils, and completely dissolves into the blue drop at your navel. Continue in that way seven or twelve times and dispel the stale winds. After that, the blue drop of wind dissolves. Draw the lower wind upward and suppress the upper winds down, five finger-widths below your navel, for a short while. With your left hand in meditative posture, take your right hand and circle your knee once, snap your fingers once, and immediately exhale slowly. Repeating this process many times establishes one short session. Again, a wind immediately emerges from the green drop of wind in the east and emerges from your nostrils, and when it reenters it immediately dissolves back into the eastern drop. Hold your breath and encircle your knee twice with your right hand and snap your fingers twice several times. This is the second small session. Visualize the yellow drop in the same way, encircle your knee three times and snap your fingers three times, which creates the third small session. Once you visualize the red drop, encircle your knee four times and snap your fingers four times, which creates the fourth small session. Once you visualize the white drop, encircle your knee five times and snap your fingers five times, which creates the fifth small session and completes one great session. Such a process of five small sessions creates one great session, and creates three great "day" sessions and three great "night" sessions. For the second great session, work with the [blue drop associated with] the wind of the space element and circle your knees and snap your fingers six times. Then do seven, eight, nine, ten transfers, and so on. In the third great session, do from eleven to fifteen transfers; in the fourth great session, do from sixteen to twenty transfers; in the fifth great session, do from twenty-one to twenty-five transfers. By practicing in that way, the person with the best faculties can complete it [i.e., the training in winds] in three days, the middling in seven days, and the least in half a month. It is taught that by increasing the strength of the wind of the fire-wind, your bodily heat increases, your ability to withstand the cold increases, your tongue becomes dry, your thirst increases, and so on.

Next is the actual stage of blessing the self. Directly in the center of your hollow red body, [which is] of the nature of light, is the central channel, with a dimension that is one-hundredth of a horse's tail hair.

It is clear red, [also] of the nature of light, and with the lower end below the navel. The upper end terminates at the Brahma aperture. To its right is the red roma channel, and to its left is the white kyangma channel. These two are the circumference of a thin stalk of wheat. They descend just beyond the lower end of the central channel, while their upper ends terminate at the openings of the nostrils. The three channels coalesce to create a single vacuole in the center of both the navel and the wheel of great bliss. At the lower end of the central channel is a red AM,[72] standing upright and of the nature of heat. At the tri-juncture is a green, bow-shaped wind mandala. At the soles of each of the two feet are red DZHEMs of the nature of a fire mandala. In the center of the single vacuole created by the three channel wheels at the crown is an upside-down white HAM. Above that is a dark-green wind [mandala] the size of a split pea, either at the back of the neck or at the crown of your head. Visualize that the HAM and the AM in the central channel are being bound together [by the DZEM syllables and the green wind mandala at the crown], and perform the nine-round breathing for dispelling stale winds. The lower winds are drawn upward by merely contracting the fingers and toes, whereby the fire-wind emerges from the two syllables at the soles of the feet, creating a turbulent combustion that enters into the large channels at the ankles and thighs. By striking the wind mandala at the tri-juncture, a turbulent wind is stirred, evoking the AM at your navel, from which a fire blazes. The fire-wind does *not* become mixed with that of the right and left channels. The wind at the crown is evoked. Draw in three small breaths from above, which enter the right and left channels. By striking the wind above the HAM, a turbulent [wind] arises from it. The entire fire-wind descends as though it is suppressed and moves downward within the right and left channels. Through that, the AM at the navel is fanned like the blowing of bellows, whereby the fire-wind blazes strongly. Imagine this and restrain the winds in the vase breath. When that generates discomfort, exhale slowly and meditate again as before. Meditate in this manner,

72. The AM and HAM are syllables created by a letter AH and letter HA each with a circle upon it that serves as a grammatical marker and represents the sound "ma," thus transforming them into the letters AM and HAM.

without counting the length of the sessions or the number of sessions. At first, you will generate heat at the abode of the navel. Next, you will generate great heat throughout your entire body. Don't concern yourself about whether the bliss that you generate at that time is ordinary bliss when that wind has entered the body. Next, the body becomes [as light] as cotton and you think, "This is the bliss of the exalted wisdom of the truth body" and generate great bliss when that wind has entered the mind. Next, generate an experience that has transcended thoughts such as "Is this bliss or isn't it?" [and] "Is this emptiness or isn't it?," and cultivate the thought that all the winds of the body, including those of the right and left channel, have entered the central channel when that wind enters the channel. At the third of these, as well as the first, you have a feeling of bliss; at the second, the bliss of nonconceptuality; at the third, it is called "the exalted wisdom illustrating the example." It is said that at that time, opening the mouth of the central channel has become serviceable. For that reason, at that time the sound of the lotus in all the channels is taught. Therefore, in this case as well, the lotus of the navel and the three channels at the level of the channel wheel at the navel become a single vacuole, with a moon-seat at the lower end. Meditate single-pointedly upon the five drops, which are the nature of the wind of the five elements in accordance with the previous explanation. By practicing the stage of cleansing the winds in this way, you make the winds serviceable.

Next, you visualize the three channels, syllables, wind mandala, and so forth. Once you fan the AM below the navel with the upper and lower winds, the fire blazes, and the winds are brought into embrace in the yoga of the vase breath and held for as long as possible. This is meditating on the stage of blessing the self.

Therefore, you are praying, "Initially, through the force of the 'mount of odor' wind entering the body, I merely generate a feeling of bliss but pay no special attention to the ordinary bliss. Next, through the force of the wind entering the mind, I imagine that bliss to be the exalted wisdom of the truth body and generate a nonconceptual bliss. Next, through the force of the wind entering the [central] channel, I generate the bliss of the exalted wisdom of the symbolic example [clear light]. In that way, may my mental continuum be satiated by great bliss."

GLORIOUS CHAKRASAMVARA

Praying for the Oral Instructions on the Yoga Inner Fire to Open the Mouth of the Central Channel

This is revealed in the dedication prayer, which states:

> When the beautiful goddess of normal-light inner fire
> With an ecstatic laugh and smile within my central channel
> Has thoroughly pleased the youthful letter HAM,
> May I attain the ground of the great bliss of union.

The three channels form a single vacuole at the level of the emanation wheel at the navel, in the center of which is an AM. Beyond that, on eight of the [sixty-four] channel wheels are the eight [syllables] A KA TSA TA THA PA YA SHA. Beyond that, on the fifty-six channel petals, are the fifty-six letters consisting of the forty [Sanskrit] consonants, the sixteen vowels, and the short vowels A I U E O A, standing upright [and] arranged counterclockwise, which are the nature of pure elements. The rest—namely, the three channels and the wind mandala at the tri-juncture, the DZHEMs at the soles of the two feet, the HAM at the crown, [and] the wind upon that at the back of the neck—are the same as in the explanation given during blessing the self.

Within the circle upon the AM at the navel is an upright red KYUM, of the nature of the ordinary [or normal] inner fire. Within the circle of the HAM at the crown is an inverted red KYUM, of the nature of the inner fire of light. Next, retract the fingers and toes, which draws the lower wind upward slightly, whereby the fire-wind at the soles of the two feet and [the wind mandala at] the tri-juncture [of the central, left, and right channels] cause the AM at the navel to blaze as before, incinerating all the impure elements. A red blaze of the nature of fire roars throughout the interior of all the channels. Next, a fierce heat of the nature of sharply pointed spokes, like particles of lightning-fire, emerges from the KYUM of normal inner fire within the circle of the AM [and] travels upward through the passageway of the central channel, [then] strikes the HAM at the crown as though it were pierced by an arrow. Inhale the upper wind through the two nostrils with three small breaths, whereby they enter through the tips of the three channels. They strike the wind at the back of the neck, whereby it is stirred, after which a blaze of fire similar to before emerges from the KYUM of the nature of inner-fire light within the circle of the HAM, which moves downward within the central channel. Through this, the fire-wind moves downward, suppressing downward all the fire-winds. The two upper and lower fire-lights meet at the level of the heart within the central channel. Focus your attention on the lights of these fires engaged in a type of combat, after which you bring the winds into embrace in a vase breath for a short while. Shake your body a little, restrain [the vase breath] to the best of your ability, and finish by repeating this a few times. The lower tongue of fire strikes the HAM, from which the white bodhichitta descends like the Kyanar River as a string of crystal and presses the upper fire-wind downward. Then you focus your mind on the blazing and dripping at the level of the heart, which is like a tangled mess of hair.

Through practicing in this way, the person of supreme faculties will be able to open the mouth of the central channel and cause the entirety of wind and mind to enter the central channel. The middling [will be able to do so] in a future life, the least through a continuity of rebirths, whereby it is said that [all three] will attain the state of union of great bliss endowed with the seven limbs.[73] Moreover, although Rigzin [Pema Trinlay] the Great states that the term "normal light" in this verse means "the completion stage of the Solitary Mother," my Venerable Guru [Ngul-chu Dharmabhadra] said that this is an elaboration on a prayer for the common completion stage of the Solitary Father. If we examine this from an honest perspective, once we bear in mind this intention, we see that there are three separate verses composed as a prayer for the completion stage of the Solitary Mother. Therefore, you are praying, "Through the force of meditating on the light rays from the normal inner fire from the lower end of the central channel and the charming light from the inner fire at the upper end within the central channel in general—and in particular the smiling and laughing light within the central channel at the heart, together with the condition of the creative play of their entanglement—may a stream of white bodhichitta created by thoroughly delighting the youthful syllable HAM at the crown of my head descend and strike the tongue of the fire created through the force of the blazing and dripping within the central channel at my heart, through which I may attain the union of great bliss before too long in this life."

Therefore, if you don't at least understand the sequence of visualizations on the path of the common central channel of the Solitary Father, you will not understand the exact meaning of these two verses. Considering this, once you establish your mind in a state of equanimity through the preliminary limbs [of practice], you will come to realize that they

---

73. The seven limbs of embrace are the qualities of an enjoyment body: 1) complete enjoyment, 2) union, 3) great bliss, 4) the lack of inherent existence, 5) completely filled with compassion, 6) uninterrupted continuity, and 7) unceasing.

have been arranged without contradicting the teachings of the previous gurus in a concise form, yet contain the essential of the visualization.

Praying to Generate the Lesser Path of the Central Channel Uncommon to the Solitary Mother has two sections:

1) PRAYING FOR THE PATH OF BEING SHOWN REALITY INDIRECTLY
2) PRAYING FOR THE PATH OF BEING SHOWN REALITY DIRECTLY

Praying for the Path of Being Shown Reality Indirectly has two sections:

1) PRAYING FOR THE PATH OF COLLECTING THE WIND AND MIND INTO THE CENTRAL CHANNEL
2) PRAYING FOR MEDITATING ON THE PATH ONCE THEY HAVE BEEN COLLECTED

Praying for the Path of Collecting the Wind and Mind into the Central Channel

This is revealed in the dedication prayer, which states:

> When the flame of the dark-red letter RAM dwelling in the center
> Of the three channels at my navel has been ignited,
> May it consume the seventy-two-thousand defiled elements
> And fill my central channel with pristine [drops].

Moreover, you should come to understand the basis, path, and result; the demarcation line of practice; the way of mistaking the essential points of the body; how to meditate on the hollow body; [and] how to visualize the three channels within the body, and so forth, in accordance with the teachings presented in the *Lecture Notes*.

For the actual practice, meditate on a reddish-black RAM together with a crescent moon, drop, and nada the size of a small globule without a cushion, abiding in the very center of the single vacuole formed by the three channels at the level of the navel that is the nature of mundane and supramundane fire. Dispel the stale winds, [then] draw the lower winds upward just slightly, after which you swallow the upper wind gently and press it downward to the navel. Retract the lower doors slightly and draw the lower winds upward with great force. And while your mind is absorbed into the syllable RAM, imagine that the upper and lower winds fan it and you restrain the winds in embrace as the vase breath. When that causes you to become uncomfortable, exhale gently through your two nostrils without letting it leave through your mouth. Restrain [the winds] exactly as before, seven times, and nourish the fire, whereby the redness of the syllable RAM increases and multitudes of red sparks emerge. Furthermore, imagine that once it increases, a slight fire-light emanates and an orange flicker spreads throughout all the vacuoles of the channels. Again, restrain the winds seven times as before, for the sake of igniting the fire, whereby the fire from the RAM continuously increases and spreads throughout all the channels, and simultaneously desiccates and incinerates all the defiled elements as well as your negative karma and obscurations. Engage in the exact same process as before seven more times, whereby all the pure upper elements melt, travel through the right and left channels, and enter the central channel, whereby the majority of the central channel is filled. The pure lower elements enter the right and left channels, and the lower ends of the right and left channels are inserted into the lower end of the central channel. Through this, the inside of the central channel, from the point between the eyebrows down to your secret place, is completely filled with the pure white element, which is a color similar to mercury, [and] through this it is filled with fire, whereby you generate great bliss. That [blissful mind] ascertains emptiness, whereby you generate the exalted wisdom of bliss and emptiness.

Through practicing in this way, the heat increases. It is explained that if it is as though [the heat] has spread between your skin and muscle, you have not penetrated the essential point [of the central channel]. If the heat is slight and is like the tip of a needle in the center of your navel, it is a sign that you have penetrated the essential point.

With respect to visualizing just the three channels, their proportions are explained in the scriptures. According to the assertion of other Gelugpas, if you happen to visualize the three channels as well as either the four or six channel wheels—whichever is most appropriate—this is best; this also applies to the great central-channel practice [of the Solitary Father].

For that reason, you are praying, "May I generate the exalted wisdom of bliss and emptiness in dependence upon pure elements filling the central channel, which is induced by bringing the upper and lower winds into embrace with the single vacuole created by the three channels at my navel, where the reddish-black-colored RAM resides whereby the pure fire is ignited. The inner fire at the navel incinerates all the impure elements within the seventy-two-thousand channels [by traveling in sequence from the heart]. Each of the eight channel petals at the heart branches out into three each, creating twenty-four; each of those branches out into three, creating seventy-two; [and] each of those branches out into a thousand, creating seventy-two thousand."

Praying for Meditating on the Path Once They Have Been Collected has two sections:

1) PRAYING TO ACCOMPLISH BLISS THROUGH THE WIND ABIDING IN THE BODY
2) PRAYING TO ACCOMPLISH EMPTINESS THROUGH THE WIND ABIDING IN THE MIND

Praying to Accomplish Bliss through the Wind Abiding in the Body

This is revealed by the dedication prayer, which states:

> When the five-colored drop between my eyebrows has gone
>   to my crown
> And a stream of moon-liquid emerges and flows
> Down to the stamen of the lotus at my secret place,
> May I be satiated by the four stable joys of ascent and descent.

Moreover, if you practice by combining with the former [meditations], other than the central channel, all the rest of the visual supports dissolve, and you perform the expelling of stale winds and meditation on the body as an empty shell just as before. The upper end of the central channel is at the point between the eyebrows, and the lower end is in the shape of a three-petaled lotus with a hole [in each one]. In the hole in the center of it [i.e., the lotus] is a white stamen with a red phenomena source at both the upper and lower tips. Within the phenomena source at the upper end [of the central channel] is a five-colored drop of sparkling colors, which is round and the size of a small pea. Through your mind entering that, you meditate between the eyebrows until you generate a feeling of bliss, itching, coldness, and so forth. Next, once you have visualized your mind as the drop in the center [of the central channel between the eyebrows], it moves to the crown of your head and comes to rest there, like a star at a mountain peak, and you meditate as before. Next, an extremely subtle drop of white bodhichitta descends from the white drop in the center [of the central channel at the crown of your head] and sequentially descends to your throat, heart, navel, and then arrives at the phenomena source at your secret place. Next, imagine the four joys of ascent, and once you have conjoined bliss and emptiness, dwell in that state for a short while. Once again, as it [i.e., the drop] repeatedly emerges three-and-a-half finger-widths from the phenomena source, imagine that you greatly increase your spontaneously born bliss. With respect to the continual increase of joy through the gradual descent of the bodhichitta, although the [amount of] water may not be great when a waterfall initially descends from the peak of a mountain, due to the condition of the upper streams coalescing, the water farther down the mountain increases [more and more]. In the same way, the joy increases through the increasing power of bodhichitta. After the bodhichitta is once again collected upward, it decreases, whereby it arrives at the navel, heart, throat, and crown and you imagine that you generate a superior four joys of ascent and descent, and you meditate once you conjoin bliss and emptiness. In particular, as the bodhichitta arrives at the secret place, generate the simultaneously born joy, although you shouldn't stabilize it for a prolonged period of time. Once the bodhichitta arrives at the crown, generate simultaneously born joy.

The phrase "At that place it is the unchanging protector" indicates that it does not change for a prolonged period of time. Moreover, as the white bodhichitta descends, three portions of the red bodhichitta also definitely descend. At that time, the yogi with supreme realizations is able to generate bliss from the red and white bodhichitta. The four joys—such as joy, supreme joy, and so forth, with four divisions each—are generated from the white bodhichitta, which equals sixteen divisions. And each of the four joys that occurs due to the red bodhichitta is divided into lesser, middling, and supreme, equaling twelve divisions of the four joys.

Next, regarding the five-colored drop between the eyebrows, it goes to the point where the central channel bends at the crown, and having arrived there, a stream of melted white bodhichitta emerges, descends like a stream of moon-liquid, and goes from the crown to the white anthers of the lotus of your secret place, which is the "descent from above." Thus you are praying, "May my mind be satiated in the nature of bliss and emptiness through the four stable joys, as it once again descends from my crown."

Praying to Accomplish Emptiness through the Wind Abiding in the Mind

This is revealed in the dedication prayer, which states:

> When I am struck with the five-colored light radiating from
> that drop,
> All things stable and moving, my body, and so forth
> Are transformed into a mass of radiant, clear rainbow [lights];
> May I once again enter into the natural abode—the sphere
> of bliss and emptiness.

Furthermore, just as before, once the drop at the bend at the crown of the head arrives at the point between your eyebrows and increasing sensation of bliss occurs, a mist of five-colored light rays radiates from it, whereby all worlds and their beings equaling the extent of space each becomes the nature of bliss and emptiness and transforms into five-colored rainbow lights. Absorb your mind into this state to the best of your ability. Next, although the previous texts state that they disappear into space, our teachings state that not only is this inappropriate during the generation stage, it is utterly inappropriate during the completion stage. Therefore, you should imagine that it [i.e., the mist] sequentially dissolves inward from the edges up to the drop, like breath dissipating on a mirror. The [drop] also dissipates into emptiness, or you focus your mind on it being the size of a mustard seed, and place your mind in the state of bliss and emptiness. [Then] repeat the same process. It is taught that through training in radiating and collecting, [and] through imagining that you accomplish these stages, certain signs of success will emerge. Next, five-colored light rays radiate from the drop abiding at your crown, and by [the rays] merely touching you, your Vajrayogini body becomes extremely transparent and so forth. The stable environment and moving [rays] all become pure and translucent and transform into a mass of five-colored rainbow lights. Once you sequentially dissolve them as before, you dwell within that previous drop. Thus you are praying, "May I be able to enter into the sphere of emptiness that is the nature of bliss and emptiness."

Praying for the Path of Being Shown Reality Directly

This is revealed in the dedication prayer, which states:

> When my mind the yogini, the union beyond intellect,
> The primordial state of emptiness and clarity beyond expression
> Recognizes its true essence—the face of its ultimate nature,
> Free from production, cessation, and abiding—may I be
>   eternally nourished.

For this, Rigzin [Pema Trinlay] the Great instructs us that you need to understand your own mind, as the secret yogini, as being the most important of the three mixings of the messengers during the generation stage. The meaning of the secret dakini is according to the commentary. Showing reality directly is like a pointing-out instruction that identifies our ultimate nature, as the example and meaning clear lights, with innate primordial mind, and whatever impedes our true nature, there is no real contradiction. However, the statement "The secret dakini is the principal of the three messengers and is the means of recognizing the ultimate basis of purification during the generation stage, with the outer yogini as the pleasing Mother of the Conquerors..." does not reveal the slightest relationship to the subsequent [practice of] the completion stage in which reality is directly revealed. Yet from the perspective of the literal meaning of the words, it is the intention of Tsarchen Dorje Chang that this means that showing reality directly is one aspect of the completion stage. This is the intended meaning of the commentary. Moreover, while showing reality directly, you place three split peas in the center of a black mandala base while the lama says, "I am revealing an instruction to you; therefore do not be distracted." He proclaims this five times, after which he takes a conch shell and stainless garment that were hidden in a cavity and suddenly places them upon the mandala and split peas. Next, you develop the three recognitions for one symbol of the true teachings, which have the three meaning of: 1) when not produced, 2) during production, and 3) post-production.

During the first, you wonder, "During the preliminary, I didn't have pure perception" and you wonder, "Just what is it that he is showing me?" He states, "Just like space, it is uncreated and not produced. Likewise, bodhichitta does not come from anywhere."

During the second, he says, "At the time of having pure perception, that conception is produced. After pure perception, it is also not produced. Just as space is produced and unproduced, so at that moment you can also not eternally remain in that state uninterruptedly."

During the third, he says, "During pure conception as well as when the pure mind has ceased, just like space, it is not continuously obstructed and is also not produced."

[The lama then continues, saying,] "The ultimate meaning of all phenomena as being unproduced is revealed through numerous analogies; therefore they ultimately do not cease. They are nondual; therefore they do not abide in the interim, either. Therefore they are free from production, ceasing, and abiding, just like space." Through coming to a decisive conclusion, the mind absorbs into and abides with the state of union.

For that reason, you are praying, "With respect to the meaning of all phenomena, such as being produced, ceasing, and abiding as being from production, ceasing, and abiding, this is the system for recognizing its true essence—the face of its ultimate nature. That emptiness and clarity is beyond expression, and the purity of emptiness and clarity dwells within 'the innate primordial mind,' or, in other words, 'the union of bliss and emptiness.' It transcends the objects of the ordinary mind, or, in other words, is 'like my guru introducing me to Vajrayogini just as she is.' Once I have recognized this, may I be continuously nourished."

When it came to this point, Je Takphu the Great said:

> Showing reality directly does not correspond to the mode of existence of the conventional mind; therefore it is essential to have the desire to have it revealed in dependence upon symbolic methods, to show that the ultimate mode of existence does not have its own characteristics of production and cessation. With respect to that, the objective emptiness is common to the Perfection Vehicle, whereas here in this practice, during the generation stage, although it is absolutely essential that the yogi meditate during the common path, he does generate a new mode of realizing the generic image [of emptiness].

And [Je Takphu also said], "The way to realize the generic image was revealed by Je Jamyang Khyentse [Wangchug, 1524–1568]." In addition, Khenchen said, "Realizing the generic image is the way of children." Therefore, the meanings of showing reality directly and showing reality indirectly are both determined from the perspective of whether or not it has developed in your mental continuum. Realizing a generic image of emptiness—and realizing it directly with simultaneously born bliss—is a unique feature of highest yoga tantra and reveals the meaning of the example and meaning clear lights and so on. If there were no distinction made, you would have to wonder what unique features it has that distinguish it from realizing emptiness in the lower systems.

Praying to Accomplish the Results of the Completion Stage

This is revealed in the dedication prayer, which states:

> When my channels, winds, and drops have dissolved into the sphere of EVAM

And [the mind] itself has attained the glorious state of the truth
   body of great bliss,
May I sustain these living beings as boundless as space
With limitless manifestations of countless form bodies.

Moreover, in this tradition, we collect the wind and mind into the central
channel, and once they are collected we meditate on the aspects of the
path adorned with oral instructions. Therefore, if we examine the way
to accomplish the rainbow body and so forth, we see that there are the
conducts in general, and in particular the outer condition of embracing
with a karma mudra as the secondary condition for accomplishing union.
The inner condition is visualizing the pervasive wind and meditating on
vajra recitation and so forth, through which all the coarse and subtle
winds enter, abide in, and dissolve into the central channel in exactly
the same way as occurs at death. During the clear light, your subjective
mind of simultaneously born bliss sequentially realizes a generic image
of emptiness and then [realizes it] directly, whereby subject and object
become one taste as you absorb your mind single-pointedly within the
state of emptiness. From there, you sequentially actualize the example
and meaning clear lights, together with the impure and pure illusory
body—the second being the union of learning. Afterward, you once
again rely upon the outer and inner conditions and attain the state of
no-more-learning endowed with the seven limbs of the union of body
and mind.

For that reason, you practice the completion stage as previously
explained, whereby the coarse and subtle wind and mind, together with
the drops within your channels, all enter, abide in, and dissolve into your
central channel. The objective wisdom of emptiness is symbolized by the
syllable EH and the objective method of great bliss is symbolized by the
syllable VAM, which become one taste of inseparability.

When the mind itself emerges from this dissolution into the sphere
of bliss and emptiness, you attain the body of the pure illusory body and
the pure mind of meaning clear light, which are unified as one entity
of body and mind as you attain the glorious body of the truth body of
great bliss. Thus you are praying, "May I emanate countless form bodies, which are simultaneously revealed in limitless manifestations for the

welfare of trainees, and care for these countless living beings filling the extent of space with compassion until I can establish them in the same state I have attained."

The Concise Meaning of the Complete Path

This is revealed in the dedication prayer, which states:

> In short, through the force of being cared for without separation
> By the Guru–Venerable Mother of Dakini Land,
> May I quickly progress along the grounds and paths, and
> By completing them, may I attain the state of the Great Dakini.

Moreover, if you condense the previous explanation of the dedication prayer into its most essential meaning, you are saying, "May I be cared for without being separated even for an instant from the guru, who reveals the general and specific aspects of this unmistaken path in dependence upon the pleasing actions of the three types of pleasing,[74] without ever being separated from the definitive meaning of the Venerable Goddess of Dakini Land. In this way, may I attain the state of the union of no-more-learning as the Great Dakini, once I have quickly perfected my progression on all the grounds and paths of sutra and tantra, in dependence upon the power of practicing with great earnestness and sincerity according to the instructions on the unmistaken complete path, with its general and specific ripening and liberating of this very Venerable Mother through its profound and vast instructions."

Proclaiming Words of Truth for the Sake of Accomplishing the Prayer

This is proclaimed in the dedication prayer, which states:

> Through the blessings of the conquerors and the wondrous
> children,

---

74. This refers to pleasing your guru with: 1) material things, 2) service, and 3) practice.

The truth of nondeceptive dependent relationship,
And the power and strength of my pure superior intention,
May everything within my pure prayer be accomplished.

Furthermore, initially you meditate for the sake of attaining enlightenment for the welfare of all living beings, whereby you actualize the wondrous mind of the mind of enlightenment. In the middle, you accumulate a vast store of the two types of merit as the cause of that, whereby you actualize the wondrous conduct. Finally, once you perfect the three aspects of completion, maturation, and purification, you engage in battle with the four maras, through which you actualize the wondrous state of a conqueror. After that, through the blessings of magnificence, [you attain] the three secrets of the buddhas together with the assembly of their bodhisattva-disciples. Although the ultimate truth of all phenomena does not have even an atom of inherent existence, the truth of the utterly nondeceptive result of each and every conventional phenomenon is unmistakenly dependent upon the [that phenomenon's] individual causes.

We pray, "May I never strive for my own happiness in the slightest, and instead accomplish the happiness of my dear mother sentient beings who, tormented by suffering, are deprived of happiness, and for the sake of dispelling their suffering, may I strive to establish them in the state of the three bodies [of a buddha] through practicing the path that surpasses that of the shravakas and pratyekabuddhas. May I quickly accomplish the result of such practices, and may the power, capacity, and strength of those three [buddha bodies] be the cause of accomplishing these words of truth in exact accordance with these beings that reside within the pure prayer."

Colophon

This commentary to the prayer entitled *The Deity's Melodious Drum Summoning One to Dakini Land* was composed by myself [Yangchen Drupai Dorje] and was based on the complete prayer for the path of Naropa's Powerful Goddess of Dakini Land, Venerable Vajrayogini, composed by Tsarchen Dorje Chang the Great, entitled *A Staircase for the Fortunate Ascending to Dakini Land.*

The Lord of the Teachings of Domé (Amdo), the embodiment of good qualities of scripture and realization who is utterly devoted solely to the ways and means of benefiting all living beings without partiality [and] who in actuality is a great bodhisattva, the Ruler Huthogtu Kelsang Thubten Trinlay Gyatso Palsangpo, sent down the strong urging that stated, "Compose a commentary to the prayer adorned with oral instructions of the guru." However, I responded with the pretense of lacking the confidence to compose it, and due to the onset of old age, my body and mind have become extremely exhausted and I have become a servant to my distractions, and due to the force of constant traveling I put it on hold. Once again, my paternal brother Hardong Tulku Rinpoche came to see me and strongly insisted that I must compose it right away. Also, presently I have a faith and devotion in this practice and have shown the aspect of undertaking a great deal of practice; therefore I hope that this composition on the Venerable Goddess of Dakini Land may be of some small benefit.

I obtained the complete lineage of empowerment, oral transmission, and instructions of this profound Dharma in dependence upon the kindness of the Lord of all Lineages and Mandalas, the Omniscient [Ngulchu] Dharmabhadra Palsangpo, who in the definitive sense is, and is inseparable from, Vajradharma. Endowed with uncontrived faith and devotion in this personal deity, I, Gelong Losang Chöphel Pelam, whose other name is Jamyang Dorje, and who is commonly referred to as Yangchen Drupai Dorje, directly listened to these teachings from the mouth of my Venerable Guru. Having forsaken numerous elaborations of scriptural quotations, I compiled notes. Whatever is not clearly set forth is due to what little I could retain in the inferior vessel of my mind. It was compiled at Ngulchu rock face at Yeru in Upper Tsang, in the small cave Namsay that is nearby the Vajra Palace Cave at Ganden Peak. It was completed when I reached my seventy-second year, in the fourteenth year of the sixty-year cycle called the Iron Dragon year [1880], during the tenth day of the waxing moon of the Purvasadha constellation [of July].

Through this composition, may all living beings equaling the extent of space continuously be cared for by the Venerable Guru.

Outline of the Text

1) Identifying the Virtue to Be Dedicated
2) The Actual Way to Dedicate the Virtue That Has Been Identified

The Actual Way to Dedicate the Virtue That has Been Identified has four sections:
1) Praying to Be Cared for by a Holy Virtuous Friend Who Is the Root of the Path
2) Praying to Generate Realizations of the Actual Path in Your Mental Continuum
3) The Concise Meaning of the Complete Path
4) Proclaiming Words of Truth for the Sake of Accomplishing the Prayer

Praying to Generate Realizations of the Actual Path in Your Mental Continuum has two sections:
1) Praying for a Fully Qualified Physical Basis as the Practitioner
2) Praying to Ripen the Mental Continuum of Those Practitioners for Realizations of the Path

Praying for a Fully Qualified Physical Basis as the Practitioner has two sections:
1) Praying to Become Fully Qualified to Be Suitable to Enter the Ripening Path
2) Praying to Become Fully Qualified to Be Suitable to Enter the Liberating Path

Praying to Become Fully Qualified to Be Suitable to Enter the Ripening Path has two sections:
1) Praying to Generate the Paths of the Small and Middling Beings in Your Mental Continuum
2) Praying to Generate the Path of a Great Being in Your Mental Continuum

Praying to Ripen the Mental Continuum of Those Practitioners for Realizations of the Path has two sections:
1) Praying to Develop Realizations of the Generation Stage in Your Mental Continuum
2) Praying to Develop Realizations of the Completion Stage in Your Mental Continuum

Praying to Develop Realizations of the Generation Stage in Your Mental Continuum has two sections:
1) Praying to Develop the Path of the Generation Stage in Your Mental Continuum
2) Praying to Accomplish the Results of the Generation Stage

Praying to Develop the Path of the Generation Stage in Your Mental Continuum has eight sections:
1) Praying for the Three Yogas of Sleeping, Rising, and Experiencing Nectar
2) Praying for the Two Yogas of the Immeasurables and the Guru
3) Praying for the Yoga of Generating Oneself as the Deity
4) Praying for the Yoga of Purifying Migrating Beings
5) Praying for the Yoga of Being Blessed by the Heroes and Heroines
6) Praying for the Yoga of Verbal Recitation and Mental Recitation
7) Praying for the Yoga of Inconceivability
8) Praying for the Yoga of Daily Actions

Praying for the Yoga of Self-Generation as the Deity has two sections:
1) Praying to Identify the Ultimate Basis of Purification and Subjugating the Dakinis
2) Praying for the Actual Self-Generation as the Deity

Praying to Accomplish the Result of the Generation Stage has two sections:

1) The Actual Prayer to Accomplish the Result of the Generation Stage
2) Praying for the Special Means of Accomplishing the Result of the Generation Stage

The Actual Prayer to Accomplish the Result of the Generation Stage has two sections:

1) Praying to Accomplish Dakini Land without Abandoning Your Body
2) Praying to Be Cared for in the Intermediate State and All Future Lives

Praying to Accomplish Dakini Land without Abandoning Your Body has two sections:

1) Those of Supreme Faculties Praying to Be Liberated through Mere Meditation and Recitation
2) Those of Middling Faculties Praying to Be Liberated in Dependence upon the Langaliya Stem

Praying for the Special Means of Accomplishing the Result of the Generation Stage has two sections:

1) Praying for the Yoga of the Quick Path of Transference of Consciousness
2) Praying for the Uncommon Yoga of Inconceivability

Praying to Generate the Realizations of the Completion Stage has two sections:

1) Praying to Generate the Realizations of the Completion Stage in Your Mental Continuum
2) Praying to Accomplish the Results of the Completion Stage

Praying to Generate the Realizations of the Completion Stage in Your Mental Continuum has two sections:

1) Praying to Generate the Great Path of the Central Channel Common to the Solitary Father
2) Praying to Generate the Lesser Path of the Central Channel Uncommon to the Solitary Mother

Praying to Generate the Great Path of the Central Channel Common to the Solitary Father has two sections:
1) Praying for the Yoga of Blessing the Self
2) Praying for the Oral Instructions on the Yoga Inner Fire to Open the Mouth of the Central Channel

Praying to Generate the Lesser Path of the Central Channel Uncommon to the Solitary Mother has two sections:
1) Praying for the Path of Being Shown Reality Indirectly
2) Praying for the Path of Being Shown Reality Directly

Praying for the Path of Being Shown Reality Indirectly has two sections:
1) Praying for the Path of Collecting the Wind and Mind into the Central Channel
2) Praying for Meditating on the Path Once They Have Been Collected

Praying for Meditating on the Path Once They Have Been Collected has two sections:
1) Praying to Accomplish Bliss through the Wind Abiding in the Body
2) Praying to Accomplish Emptiness through the Wind Abiding in the Mind

PART 2:

Prayers and Supplication

The Complete Prayer for the Path of Venerable Vajrayogini, Naropa's Powerful Goddess of Dakini Land, Entitled *A Staircase for the Fortunate Ascending to Dakini Land*

The Complete Prayer for the Path of Venerable Vajrayogini

BY TSARCHEN LOSAL GYATSO

Thus, through the power of meditating properly on the perfect
    liberating path
Of the Powerful Goddess of Dakini Land, the Mother of the
    Conquerors,
May I properly please the qualified guru—the source of
    attainments—
And come under his [or her] care without ever being apart.

May I be liberated from this terrifying ocean of samsara
In the great ship of freedoms and endowments,
Flying the white sail of being mindful of impermanence and
Blown by the favorable winds of adopting and forsaking cause and
    effect.

Through the influential force of compassion for mother sentient
    beings,
May I don the armor of the magnificent bodhichitta,
Enter the deep ocean of the bodhisattva's deeds,
And become a suitable vessel for the ripening empowerment.

Through the kindness of the qualified vajra-holder,
May I become a suitable vessel for meditating on the liberating path
Through enjoying the glorious nectar-blessings of
The highest yoga tantra empowerments and the Venerable Mother.

By properly protecting the vows and commitments I received
At that time as I would my eyeballs, as well as
The yogas of sleeping, rising, and experiencing nectar,
May my three doors delight in the three joys.

Relying upon the nondeceptive objects of refuge as my crown-jewel,
With the great purpose of mother sentient beings dwelling in my
    heart,
And cleansing the stains of my transgressions with the nectar of
    Vajrasattva,
May I be nurtured by the compassionate Venerable Guru.

The outer yogini is the ravishing Mother of the Conquerors,
The supreme inner Vajra Queen is the letter BAM,
The secret dakini is clarity and emptiness of the nature of mind;
May I delightfully partake in seeing their true identity.

May I complete the yoga of generating myself as the deity,
The supreme ripening agent for developing realizations of the path and
    result,
As the wondrous method of bringing the basis of purification—
Death, the intermediate state, and rebirth—into the path of the three
    bodies.

The worldly environment is the celestial mansion of the letter EH,
The sentient beings who inhabit them are the yoginis of the syllable
    BAM;
Through the concentration of the great bliss union [of EVAM],
May whatever appears arise as pure appearances.

Visualizing my inner channels as the thirty-seven deities,
Dissolving all phenomena of samsara and nirvana into the nature
Of the three messengers, and wearing the armor of the
    mantra-syllables,
May I never be disrupted by outer and inner interferences.

Through verbal and mental recitation focused single-pointedly upon
The mantra circles at the dharma wheel and emanation wheel,
And the two incidental completion-stage messengers,
May I induce simultaneously born bliss and emptiness.

May my mind abide in the sphere of bliss and emptiness when,
Through the lasso light rays emanating from the syllable BAM and
 mantra rosary,
The worlds and their beings of the three realms melt into light and
 dissolve into me,
And I also sequentially dissolve into emptiness.

When I arise from that in the form of the deity marked by armor,
Protected from all obstacles by the beating sounds in the directions,
May whatever appears arise as the three secrets of the deity,
And may I complete the daily actions and their branches.

Thus, through the yoga of the directions and the moon,
One day, may I be led directly to the City of Knowledge-Holders
By the coral-colored goddess of joy with free-flowing
Vermillion hair and moving orange eyes.

Practicing in a land of corpses with a langali[ya] stem filled
With sindhura, and wandering throughout all the lands,
May the beautiful goddess to whom the joy-swirl
Between my eyebrows transfers lead me to Dakini Land.

Even if I am not liberated in this life, through the force of
Applying myself single-pointedly in meditation, recitation, and
 so forth,
May the Joyous Goddess of Dakini Land take me under her care
During the intermediate state or before too long.

When the "mount of odor" wind quickly moves my mind, in the
 form a syllable BAM,
Up my central channel and through the door of Brahma,

May I attain instant liberation through the death-time path
Of mixing with the Mother of the Conqueror's mind of bliss and
   emptiness.

When the inner Varahi has destroyed the creeping vine of appre-
   hender and apprehended,
And the dancing goddess dwelling within my supreme central channel
Exits the crown of my head into the sphere of space,
May she frolic in embrace with the Hero Blood-Drinker.

Through the yoga of embrace while meditating single-pointedly
Upon the seed of the five winds at the lotus of my navel,
May my mental continuum be satiated by supreme bliss
Through the wind entering the channels of my body-mind.

When the beautiful goddess of normal-light inner fire
With an ecstatic laugh and smile within my central channel
Has thoroughly pleased the youthful letter HAM,
May I attain the ground of the great bliss of union.

When the flame of the dark-red letter RAM dwelling in the center
Of the three channels at my navel has been ignited,
May it consume the seventy-two-thousand defiled elements
And fill my central channel with pristine [drops].

When the five-colored drop between my eyebrows has gone to my
   crown
And a stream of moon-liquid emerges and flows
Down to the stamen of the lotus at my secret place,
May I be satiated by the four stable joys of ascent and descent.

When I am struck with the five-colored light radiating from that drop,
All things stable and moving, my body and so forth
Are transformed into a mass of radiant, clear rainbow [lights];
May I once again enter into the natural abode—the sphere of bliss
   and emptiness.

When my mind the yogini, the union beyond intellect,
The primordial state of emptiness and clarity beyond expression
Recognizes its true essence—the face of its ultimate nature,
Free from birth, cessation, and abiding—may I be eternally
    nourished.

When my channels, winds, and drops have dissolved into the sphere
    of EVAM
And [the mind] itself has attained the glorious state of the truth body
    of great bliss,
May I sustain these living beings as boundless as space
With limitless manifestations of countless form bodies.

In short, through the force of being cared for without separation
By the Guru–Venerable Mother of Dakini Land,
May I quickly progress along the grounds and paths, and
By completing them may I attain the state of the Great Dakini.

Through the blessings of the conquerors and the wondrous children,
The truth of nondeceptive dependent relationship,
And the power and strength of my pure superior intention,
May everything within my pure prayer be accomplished.

COLOPHON

This is the complete dedication prayer of Venerable Vajrayogini, the
Powerful Goddess of Dakini Land, entitled *A Staircase for the Fortunate
Ascending to Dakini Land*. It was composed by Tsarchen Dorje Chang Losal
Gyatso Palsangpo. At the conclusion of his dedication prayer it states,
"This request to Venerable Vajrayogini—Naropa's Goddess of Dakini
Land—and the lineage gurus is entitled *A Festival of Laughing Lotuses*.
Relying on the exalted and special words and meaning of this prayer has
unimaginably great power to bring blessing to this 'great ship of leisure
and endowment.' This system has been the practice of numerous previous
gurus. Although the tradition is to recite the prayer at the end of your
practice, it is partially a request of this lineage; therefore, although being

brief, there is nothing better to rely upon. While establishing my aspiration to compose a commentary to this, I followed a system that accords with the praise as a request to the guru and the Venerable Goddess of Dakini Land. It was compiled by the person named Yangchen Drupai Dorje during a good year, during the eighteenth day of the twenty-fifth lunar mansion, during the waning moon at the Vajra Palace, in a cave on the peak of Ganden Mountain in Ngulchu Hermitage."

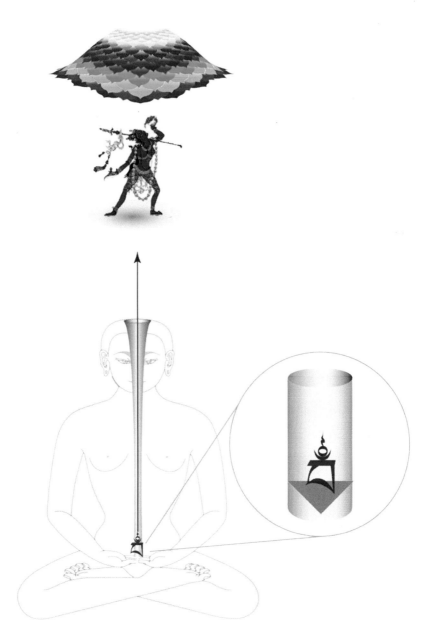

Transference of Consciousness of the Solitary Mother
(Courtesy of Wolfgang Saumweber)

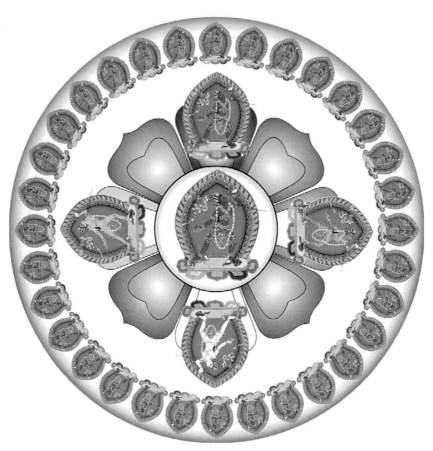

Body Mandala Deities *Within* the Central Channel

(Courtesy of Wolfgang Saumweber)

A Praise and a Supplication to Venerable
Vajrayogini Composed in Verse, Entitled
A Hook Summoning Swift Attainments

A Praise to Venerable Vajrayogini

BY YANGCHEN DRUPAI DORJE

NAMO GURU CHAKRASAMVARA YA

I prostrate to Glorious Heruka Father and Mother.
As a powerful mountainous heap of sapphire,
Your captivating body is as though embraced by youthful clouds.
Merely remembering you bestows great bliss.

As the play of unchanging simultaneously born joy,
You act to generate delight in the Supreme Hero;
Venerable Vajrayogini the powerful dakini,
I praise you with a powerful mind of faith.

A blazing heap of five exalted wisdoms,
[You are] invincible within your vast vajra-tent abode,
Dwelling amidst the encircling, terrifying, and dreadful
Eight great charnel grounds that completely envelop it.

Free of emptiness, signlessness, and wishlessness, abiding in the
Dharma source of all—the exalted wisdom of great bliss of equal
    taste—
With a broad, raised cobra hood of good qualities,
Your whirling drops of the four joys spin counterclockwise.

In the center of that is a lotus-seat free from the faults of samsara.
Upon a swirling crystal of the nature of bodhichitta

Is the Bhagavati whose body is insatiable to view, and
Whose exalted wisdom outshines the rays of the sun.

Your great compassion is the nature of simultaneously born
Great bliss and cares for migrators with affection.
As a blazing mountain, the color of a ruby,
It is as though you are embraced by a hundred-thousand
   youthful suns.

Your face reveals the single taste of the two truths' union
That penetrates wisdom's sphere of emptiness, through which
The supremely fortunate are lead to inner Dakini Land
As though you are instructing them, "I am the one who will lead
   you there!"

Through unifying method and wisdom, your
Feet are like supple branches of ruby in a stance of
Outstretched and bent, treading on Kalarati and Bhairava,
 As a sign revealing that you have transcended the extremes of exis-
   tence and nonexistence, permanence and annihilation.

Your outstretched hand holds a wisdom-curved knife of compassion
That is the union of method and wisdom, symbolizing that you
Cut through the net of conceptions grasping at extremes
And sever all the faults of samsara from their very source.

Although you have attained peace, the might of
Your compassion never wavers from the welfare of others, and
Your hand of wisdom with the bliss-sustaining vessel filled with
The taste of compassion lifts them to the state of nirvana.

To symbolize that you are never separate from
The wisdom of emptiness and the method of great bliss,
You embrace Glorious Heruka in the crook of your
Left arm in the form of a katvanga.

Your upper body is covered by your mass of shiny black hair,
Flowing freely because you are liberated from the demon of
    self-grasping.
Because you are satiated by an abundant increase of the sixteen joys,
You reveal the blooming, charming beauty of a sixteen-year-old.

Your desirous breasts with narrow cleavage are voluptuous,
And a stream of blood drips from your secret lotus;
Your revealing aspect is a treasure intoxicating the hearts
Of the fortunate with the nectar of simultaneously born great bliss.

The nature of your body is nectar, adorning the eyes.
You wear a crown ornament the nature of the five Sugatas
As the method aspect of the five perfections such as giving
    and so on,
While the appearance of your five bone ornaments is the perfection
    of wisdom.

Your pure inner vowels and consonants are
At one with your fifty hanging skulls.
The corpse-thread is your realization of wisdom
That binds your long, hanging necklace.

With Vairochana-Heruka as your crown ornament,
And your perception of the equality of all phenomena,
You abide in the center of a blazing, swirling mass of light rays
As the fire of the eon that is the manifestation of your exalted
    wisdom.

Thus the Virtuous Goddess of the perfection of wisdom is the Mother
    of the Conquerors,
Arising as a magical display of all things within samsara and nirvana
Appearing in the body of a beautiful goddess. Venerable Mother,
When I recall you from the depths of my heart and make
    supplications,

You arise from the sphere of the clear light in that form.
When the collection of small bells hanging from your skirt is stirred
    by the breeze,
Your dancing posture causes them to produce a delightful sound
That is supplicating us to "Come this way, come to the festival of
    bliss."

By revealing your smiling face like a broad lotus,
Your desirous sideways glance grabs us with its noose-like rays.
Your delightful lips are red like a bimba[75] fruit;
Please bestow upon me the hundred flavors of your honey.

You openly proclaim your melodious song with sixteen melodies,
You reveal your skill in the sixty-four arts of love
And unite with the male organ as the secret abode of the dakinis,
A treasure satiating my mind with the four joys of embrace.

Delighted by the supreme maiden of the sixteen joys
Induced by the blazing and dripping of AH and HAM,
You are a treasure multiplying the emanated festival of skillful means
That robs samsara and nirvana of their torments.

Through the force of that, once I quickly perfect the journey of
The path unifying the illusory body and clear light,
Please bestow upon me the good fortune of actualizing
The vajra-body of union in this very life.

Just as you cared for countless fortunate yogis
Of India, such as Vajra Ghantapa,
Kusali, Naropa, and so forth,
May the Powerful Goddess of Dakini Land care for me in the
    same way.

---

75. The bimba fruit is something akin to a red cherry.

Just as you successively cared for Pamtingpa, Purang Lotsawa,
The supreme siddhas of Glorious Sakya,
And in particular Tsarchen Father and Sons,
May the Powerful Goddess of Dakini Land care for me in the
    same way.

In particular, just as you cared for the Supreme Guide
[Ngulchu] Dharmabhadra Shab, by empowering him
As the lord of the stainless Hearing Lineage,
May the Powerful Goddess of Dakini Land care for me in the
    same way.

COLOPHON

These verses were composed by Yangchen Drupai Dorje according to
the request of Gelong Ngawang Tendar, who said they were needed.

A Hook Summoning Swift Attainments

BY TUKEN LOSANG CHÖKYI NYIMA

Keep us under your protection right now, in this very instant!
With my mind single-pointedly concentrating on your body
And my efforts in proclaiming the recitation of profound Secret
    Mantra,
Why would you reveal only a minute sign of your blessing?

Please reveal the truth of the nondeceptive teachings
Of the King of Tantras Chakrasamvara, which state that
If you apply yourself with confidence, "You will reach attainments
By merely reciting the close-essence [mantra]."

Tightly bound by the chains of karma and afflictive emotions,
I have fallen into samsara's blazing pit of suffering.
As I cry out in extreme torment, I wonder,
"Has your compassion disappeared?"

If I don't have the good fortune to perceive your supreme body of
    exalted wisdom,
Once I receive assistance on the path of a messenger through
Ordinary means, by meeting a karma mudra,
Please establish me in the supreme festival of great bliss.

If, because of a thick covering of karma, afflictions, and obscurations,
I don't have the good fortune to meet you in this life,

When I am raised up high in my next rebirth,
May you perfectly reveal your perfect face as the Venerable Goddess.

May there never arise the suffering of disturbing the elements
That bring an end to life, or the terrifying mistaken appearances of
    attachment and anger.
Grant your blessing that I may mix my mind with the
Sphere of your mind through the practice of phowa.

At that time, may the assembly of heroes and dakinis
Lead me to the Pure Dakini Land amidst an escort of
Vajra-songs, pleasing clouds of offerings,
And numerous amazing and excellent visions.

There, may the heroes and yoginis
Frolic in the ecstatic dance of simultaneously born great bliss
And reveal a limitless array of magical emanations
Filling the vast pure and impure realms.

Before too long, may I actualize the supreme state
Of the Pervasive Lord Heruka,
Eternally care for my dear mothers with kindness,
And liberate them from the great suffering of samsara.

In the meantime, please bestow the auspiciousness of
Accomplishing the supreme path and, never being overcome by outer
    and inner obstacles,
May I attract field-, mantra-, and spontaneously born assistants
And ignite the festival of bliss.

Through whatever power, strength, and capacity the protectors
    possess,
Such as the Lord of Tent, Four-Faced Mahakala, [and] the Lords of
    the Charnel Grounds,
May they never waver in fulfilling their oaths and accomplish
All pacifying, increasing, controlling, and wrathful actions.

Through the force of the blessings of Guru-Heruka,
The power and strength of the protector Legden Nagpo,
And the power of pure superior intention of myself the yogi,
May all of these desired aims be spontaneously accomplished.

Colophon

This pure canonical description of Venerable Vajrayogini's path, as well as the praise that perfectly reveals a supplication for desired aims, is entitled *A Hook Summoning Swift Attainments*. It was composed by Kusali Dharmavajra [i.e., Tuken Losang Chökyi Nyima (1737–1802)], who attained stable devotion for this path during the special time of the tenth day of the ninth month of the Iron Dog year [1790]. It was composed during the session breaks of virtuous conduct. It was compiled so that the intelligent Ngawang Tenphel may swiftly come under the care of Venerable Vajrayogini.

Glossary

Action tantra: The first of the four classes of tantra, which emphasizes external actions and utilizes gazing at a physical consort as a means of generating a blissful subjective awareness used to penetrate the nature of reality.

Basis, path, and result: Three points in time that are sequentially interrelated and transformed through a series of symbioses. The basis is our current body, speech, and mind that function as the foundation. The path is the means of transforming those three states through spiritual practice. The result occurs when the mind becomes the truth body, the speech becomes the enjoyment body, and the body becomes the emanation body.

Bodhichitta: The intention to become enlightened for the welfare of all living beings, motivated by love and compassion that see the suffering nature of samsara and seek to liberate all living beings from it.

Bodhisattva: An individual who has generated bodhichitta and has entered the path to enlightenment.

Buddha Shakyamuni: The historical Buddha, who lived approximately twenty-five hundred years ago and who was the founder of the Buddhism practiced today.

Channels: A channel is a passageway through which the winds and drops move. There are three primary channels: the central, right, and left. The ultimate goal of all highest yoga tantra practices is to bring the winds into the central channel and utilize the most subtle mind of clear light to realize the ultimate nature of reality.

Channel wheels (Skt. *chakra***):** Centers that branch out from the central channel at various points in the body and allow for the movement of energy winds throughout the body. The four main channel wheels are at the crown, the throat, the heart, and the navel. Other important channel wheels are located at the secret place, the tip of the sex organ, and at the forehead between the eyes.

Clear light: The extremely subtle mind that becomes manifest during the completion stage of highest yoga tantra and is utilized to realize emptiness.

Commitment being: A visualized buddha that can either be oneself generated as a buddha or a buddha in the space before oneself, so named because it is a commitment of tantra to visualize the buddha. It is juxtaposed to the "wisdom being" that is invoked and dissolved into the commitment being, thus rendering them inseparable.

Completion stage: The second stage of highest yoga tantra, which utilizes channels, winds, and drops to cause the winds to enter, abide in, and dissolve into the central channel, whereby one manifests subtle levels of consciousness while conjoining them with bliss, which ultimately results in actually attaining the three buddha bodies that were merely imagined during the generation stage. The five stages of natural progression that occur as a person gains higher realizations of the completion stage are: isolated speech, isolated mind, clear light, illusory body, and union.

Daka: A male enlightened being that assists tantric practitioners to accomplish realizations of Secret Mantra.

Dakini: A female enlightened being that assists tantric practitioners to accomplish realizations of Secret Mantra.

Damaru: A small ritual hand-drum played at the level of the navel that serves as both a musical offering and a means of invoking the blessings of the dakinis, to absorb them into the inner fire at the navel.

Deity: There are both mundane and supramundane deities. A mundane deity is any god or goddess that has not attained either liberation or enlightenment. A supramundane deity is either a bodhisattva on one of the three final grounds or a buddha visualized in the aspect of a particular deity.

Dharma: The teachings of the historical Buddha Shakyamuni that lead one through spiritual paths culminating in varying degrees of happiness, from the happiness of this life to the happiness of liberation and enlightenment.

Divine pride: The pride of being an enlightened being that is generated by dissolving one's ordinary aggregates and its sense of identity, and replacing them with the "divine" pride of being the deity. This entire process is utilized to strengthen one's realization of emptiness by realizing that the "I" is merely imputed.

Drops: The drops are the subtle elements of the body that course through the channels within the body in dependence upon the movement of the inner energy that flows throughout the channels. The drops can be used to generate extraordinary blissful states of mind used to penetrate the nature of reality.

Emanation body: A coarse form body of an enlightened being that is emanated for the welfare of ordinary beings.

Empowerment (Tib. *wang*): A ritual utilizing a mandala that transmits the blessing of a particular buddha in the aspect of a deity and establishes the imprints to attain the resultant body, speech, and mind of that deity.

Enjoyment body: The subtle body of an enlightened being that can be perceived only by bodhisattvas who have attained the path of seeing and beyond.

Five buddha families: Five buddhas that represent the five aggregates of an enlightened being— Akshobya as consciousness, Ratnasambhava as feeling, Amitabha as discrimination, Amoghasiddhi as compositional factors, and Vairochana as form.

Four joys: Four increasingly blissful states of consciousness that are developed through melting the white drop at the crown. As the drop flows through the central channel from the crown to the throat one develops joy, from the throat to the heart one develops supreme joy, from the heart to the navel one develops extraordinary joy, and when the white drop reaches the tip of the sex organ one develops simultaneously born joy.

Generation stage: A term unique to highest yoga tantra, where one imagines transforming the basic experience of ordinary death, the intermediate state, and rebirth into the truth body, enjoyment body, and emanation body, respectively. Although there is self-generation as the deity in the lower classes of tantra, the lower tantras don't bring the three basic experiences into the path as the three bodies of a buddha.

Heroes and heroines: Male and female tantric deities that assist tantric practitioners to attain realizations.

Highest yoga tantra: The highest of the four classes of tantra. It emphasizes internal actions and utilizes embracing a physical consort as a means of generating the most subtle mind of clear light as a blissful subjective awareness that is capable of penetrating the nature of reality.

Illusory body: The subtle body that is actualized during the completion stage. There are two divisions of the illusory body, pure and impure. The impure illusory body is attained after the attainment of ultimate example clear light, and is so called because the wind from which it is composed is still impure in the sense that the mind from which it arose has yet to directly realize emptiness. The pure illusory body is so called because it arises from meaning clear light that has directly realized emptiness.

Indestructible drop: The most subtle drop located within the heart channel wheel. It is composed of the essence of red and white drops obtained from the mother and father at the time of conception. It is also the abode of the most subtle mind of clear light that must be accessed to attain enlightenment.

Inner offering: There are two types of inner offering. The main inner offering contains a blessed pill called a "nectar pill" that is placed in a liquid, blessed, and offered to the guests. It is called the "inner offering" because the nectar pill is made of substances that represent the inner substances of living beings, and the same substances are visualized during the blessing of the inner offering itself. The second type is so called because the recipient is offered the inner tactile sense of an offering goddess.

Intermediate state (Tib. *bardo*): The transitional state between the end of one life and the beginning of the next. The intermediate state can last up to forty-nine days and consists of seven minor transitional periods, each resulting in a "small death" after which one either takes rebirth or assumes another intermediate state body.

Karma: The cause-and-effect relationship between an action created and its corresponding result: whatever we experience is a result of our previous actions. Pleasant experiences stem from virtuous actions and painful experiences stem from nonvirtuous actions.

Karma mudra: A physical consort utilized to actualize the most subtle mind of clear light through completion-stage techniques of highest yoga tantra.

Katvanga: A staff marked with various implements that represent the complete mandala of Chakrasamvara and is held in the crook of Vajra-yogini's left arm symbolizing that she is inseparable from Chakrasamvara.

Langaliya: A tree that is similar in appearance to bamboo. Its stem is used in very advanced practices of Vajrayogini at the conclusion of a "great retreat" of ten million mantras.

Mahasiddhas: Tantric adepts of varying degrees of realization who have attained a degree of realization far beyond that of an ordinary being. They are most often associated with ancient India.

Mantra: In the interpretive sense, a mantra is a set sequence of syllables used to invoke the blessings of a particular deity. In the definitive sense, a mantra is the audible expression of the particular qualities of an enlightened being's mind of bliss and emptiness.

Nada: A small, three-curved line that sits at the uppermost position of the syllable BAM and represents the three subtle minds of white appearance, red increase, and black near-attainment.

Nagarjuna: The founder of Mahayana Buddhism, who is said to have traveled to the subterranean land of the nagas to obtain the Perfection of Wisdom sutras. (A naga is a serpent-like being that has varying degrees of power that can be either malevolent or benign.)

Outer offering: A ritual offering consisting of various "outer" substances such as water, flowers, incense, and so forth.

Phenomena source: Either a single or double tetrahedron that is used in Vajrayogini practice and that symbolizes, among other things, emptiness, and represents emptiness being the source of all phenomena.

Renunciation (Tib. *nges 'byung*): Literally, "definite emergence"; refers to the "definite" determination to be liberated, or "emerge," from samsara through a proper understanding of its shortcomings.

Root downfall: A violation of one of the root vows associated with either the pratimoksha, bodhisattva, or tantric codes of discipline.

Samsara: A cycle of uncontrolled rebirth through the force of afflicted actions and delusions.

Self-grasping: Grasping at an inherently existent self, based on a mistaken interpretation of the nature of reality, which is the cause of samsara and all the suffering within it.

Seven limbs of embrace: The seven qualities unique to the enjoyment body of an enlightened being. They are: 1) complete enjoyment body, 2) union, 3) great bliss, 4) the absence of inherent existence, 5) being completely filled with great compassion, 6) unbroken continuity, and 7) ceaselessness.

Sindhura: A red powder that is sacred to both Hinduism and tantric Buddhism. It is utilized in the Vajrayogini practice as a medium for transmitting and receiving her blessings.

Sutra: A series of public discourses given by the historical Buddha Shakyamuni.

Three bodies of a buddha: The truth body, the enjoyment body, and the emanation body. See the entry for "Generation stage" above.

Three buddha families: A method for presenting the lineages, or "families," of enlightened beings as three families, where Akshobya represents the mind, Amitabha represents the speech, and Vairochana represents the body. See also "Five buddha families" above.

Transference of consciousness (Skt. *phowa*): A method to intentionally separate the subtle wind and mind from the coarse aggregates at the time of death as a means of taking rebirth in a pure land of a buddha.

Truth body (Skt. *dharmakaya*): The extremely subtle mind of an enlightened being that is completely free from the obstructions to omniscience and that serves as the foundation for the enjoyment and emanation bodies.

Tsok offering (Skt. *ganachakra*): A tantric feast involving ritual music and sacred substances for invoking the blessing of the dakas and dakinis and strengthening your tantric commitments.

Tsongkhapa: A Tibetan lama who lived 1357–1419. He is responsible for the formation of the Gelug tradition of Tibetan Buddhism. He was a great nonsectarian teacher who assembled various practices and lineages that resulted in the Gelug tradition.

Ultimate reality: The ultimate of all phenomena is their being empty of inherent existence.

Union: There are several types of union: 1) the union of bliss and emptiness at either the generation or completion stage—most notably the latter; 2) the union of the illusory body and clear light, 3) the union of learning; and 4) the union of no-more-learning. The third one is synonymous with the union of the pure illusory body and meaning clear light, and the fourth is synonymous with enlightenment.

Vairochana: One of the members of the five buddha families; he is white in color and holds a wheel and a bell. He is a physical representation of the purified aggregate of form.

Vajradhara: An emanation of Buddha Shakyamuni who appeared as a blue-colored deity and taught the various tantras.

Vajradharma: An aspect of Buddha Amitabha that is equivalent to Vajradhara and serves as the basis upon which a Vajrayogini practitioner identifies his or her spiritual guide.

Vajra-master: A highly realized lama who is skilled in tantric rituals.

Vajra recitation: The ultimate form of mantra recitation where one combines the movement of one's internal energy winds with the with the resonance of the three syllables OM, AH, HUM, whereby one's body, speech, and mind are blessed and become progressively unified with the body, speech, and mind of all enlightened beings. One's winds become inseparable from mantra, the channel knots are loosed, and the winds are brought into the indestructible drop at the heart.

Vajrasattva: A white-colored deity who is the embodiment of the purification powers of all enlightened beings.

Winds: There are coarse, subtle, and very subtle internal winds that are associated with human beings. The coarsest wind is our breath. The subtle wind functions to allow the movement of drops—or vital essences—within our body. The very subtle wind is inseparable from our very subtle mind, which ultimately transform into the truth body and the enjoyment body, respectively.

Wisdom being: The actual mind of an enlightened being that is summoned to dissolve into the commitment being.

Yoga tantra: The third of the four classes of tantra. It places primary emphasis upon internal actions and utilizes holding hands with a physical consort as a means of generating a blissful subjective awareness used to penetrate the nature of reality.

Index